ETHUEN YOUNG DRAMA

he aim of this series is to offer a range of new plays for young people. Different mes present material written for different age groups, drawn from the anding repertoire now being created by a number of modern playwrights and ariety of youth theatre companies and groups, both professional and amateur. ch play is prefaced by an account of the original conception and performance d suggestions are given for future presentation.

HE ADVENTURES OF GERVASE BECKET or The Man Who Changed Places

as written by Peter Terson specially for the company of the Victoria Theatre, toke-on-Trent. It was first performed there under the direction of Peter heeseman, who explains his approach in his introduction to the script. Set in ne early nineteenth century, the play chronicles the extraordinary saga of the entle squire Gervase Becket 'who heard a sermon and took a journey and was ever the same man again.' Accompanied by his fat, faithful and very reluctant riend Chunter, Gervase wanders across the world encountering — among other nings — robbery by highwaymen, abduction by a press-gang, the front lines of ne Spanish War, a wedding, a slave ship and the gallows. His experiences, filled ith humour, colourful characters and lively music, are guaranteed to entertain oung audiences — and anyone else who can stand the pace. Though originally aged by adults, the play is equally suitable for performance by a young cast.

D1382197

THE ADVENTURES OF GERVASE BECKET

or The Man Who Changed Places

A Play by Peter Terson

Edited with an
Introduction by
Peter Cheeseman

First published in Great Britain 1973
by Eyre Methuen Ltd
11 New Fetter Lane London EC4P 4EE
Copyright © 1973 Peter Terson
Introduction copyright © 1973 Peter Cheeseman
Fanfare music copyright © 1973 Stuart Johnson
Journey music copyright © 1973 Jeff Parton

Set by Expression Typesetters
Printed in Great Britain by
Fletchers & Sons Ltd, Norwich

SBN 413 30600 3 net edition
      423 80300 X school edition

AUTHOR'S NOTE FROM THE ORIGINAL PROGRAMME

Last year I was reading a volume of old magazines of the 1800's from a small seaport called Whitby. It was full of tales of adventure and olden times; of soldiers who drew lots to decide who could take their wives overseas; of galley slaves who were thrown overboard when their days of usefulness were over; of pursued highwaymen; of gluttons whose greed had made them unable to move; of Spanish Wars and pressmen; of criminals on scaffolds and of duststorms descending on battlefields.

I thought that if only a man could pass through all of these adventures like a brave Don Quixote what a super play it would make. So, I thought, one Sunday a contented satisfied squire heard the Vicar preach: 'Happy is the man who is content with his lot; but the man who is not content with his lot he has a thorn in his side. Let us not be vainglorious, envying one another, but let us be content with our lot. And if you meet anyone who is dissatisfied, why then, change places. That is the challenge to the contented man.'

Sir Gervase Becket takes the Vicar at his word and sets off. I hope his extraordinary adventures make an exciting play for you.

Peter Terson

INTRODUCTION

This play was written for the Victoria Theatre in Stoke-on-Trent which is a theatre in the round, with the audience on all four sides of a stage 22 feet wide and 26 feet long. There are three entrances to the stage in the form of short corridors through the audience.

At Stoke we make a habit of doing plays where there are a lot of scenes and with the action shifting all over the place and THE ADVENTURES OF GERVASE BECKET was written to get a lot of excitement out of journeys and changing scenes. We never use much scenery. The actors and the events in the story tell you where you are. But we do often enjoy using sound effects and lighting and simple bits and pieces of scenery to add to the impression of being in one place or another.

The play can be performed with any arrangement of the audience and the stage though I think it's a pity to do it in the old-fashioned way with the actors all on the headmaster's platform and us all staring at them through a hole in the wall.

The only important thing is for all the audience to be able to see and hear all the parts of the play. Incidentally you don't need to be able to see actors' faces all the time if you don't use the old-fashioned 'proscenium' arrangement. As long as you can hear the actors and see them it's a really exciting way of doing a play, for those in it as well as the audience.

You can do THE ADVENTURES OF GERVASE BECKET . . . with the audience all round the actors

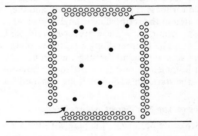

or on either side

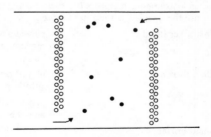

In a long hall with the acting area in the middle you can use the stage to sit on. It's a good rule *never to have more than two rows of seats on the same level,* whichever arrangement you use. So if you use more, find ways of raising them higher as they get further back.

You might like to try an arrangement like the Greek or Elizabethan stages — with the audience on three sides. People are gradually coming to see that all arrangements of actors and audiences work, and that anywhere the actors are close to the audience, and partially or totally surrounded by them, tends to be more exciting than the sort where you're just facing one another in two straight lines.

Scenery for Sir Gervase

The theatre arrangement you decide on will affect the scenery you choose, but whatever system it is will have to be simple, or mobile, or re-arrangeable quickly, or all of these, so that you can get from one scene to the other. Some simple object will help to establish the new place. In an open space, like on the journeys, it's a good idea to have it empty. I'll go through the play in a moment and make short suggestions about each scene.

Music for the Play

At Stoke we used two sorts of music — very noisy bugle and drum fanfares written by Stuart Johnson, and music for voices, autoharp and guitar by Jeff Parton for Sir Gervase's decisions to change places and for his journeys. The music for these is printed at the end, and the places where we put them in are indicated in the script. The changing places music was a set of several long chords strummed by the actress who said 'Sir Gervase Becket, change places . . . ' etc. The Journey Song was started on the autoharp, and sung to 'la' by the actors standing round the stage, watching Sir Gervase on his journey. Some bits were hummed and others whistled for variation and a guitar joined the autoharp after the start. This Journey Song was used for the dance at the end.

Notes on the Number of Actors Needed

At Stoke we performed the play with ten actors and four actresses. Everybody but the actors playing Sir Gervase and Chunter played a lot of parts, as well as musical instruments, members of crowds, congregations, peasants and so on. Here are the main parts the actors played:

Christopher Bond	played a Soldier, one of the Glutton's servants, the Arab Galley Captain and the bugle
Gillian Brown	played the Fiery Girl, Amelia and the autoharp
Alan David	played the Vicar, the Polite Sergeant and one of Sylvette's servants
Ronald Forfar	played the Highwayman, Sergeant

	Broadwhiskers, the Priest and the Executioner
Susan Glanville	played the Farm Girl and the bugle
Tim Hardy	played the Officer, an English soldier and the bugle
John Keogh	played the Glutton, the Pressgang Officer, Manuel and the Captain of the English ship
Geoffrey Larder	played Sir Gervase Becket
Christopher Martin	played the Beggar, the Innkeeper, the Count, the Criminal and the bugle
Carol Mason	played Dolly Triplefoot
Susan Tracy	played Sylvette
Christopher Whitehouse	played the one-legged Nobleman, the Champ, Blind Lumba and a drum
Arthur Whybrow	played Chunter
Brian Young	played Grimthorpe, Tommy Triplefoot, Sylvette's Father and a drum

It could be done by fewer people, and certainly by more.

Time of the Play

The play is meant to take place at the beginning of the nineteenth century, strictly speaking when the English army was fighting Napoleon in Spain and when the Press Gangs were operating to get sailors for the Navy. The actors wore costumes that looked right for this. Peter Terson's drawings in this book also give a good idea of the kind of clothes that could be worn.

Scenery

The scenery consisted of wooden slatted crates of various shapes and sizes including some low ones like small rostra on castors that we could wheel on and off. The crates were like big child's building blocks in that you could put them together in different ways to make a pulpit, a bar, a hatch on a ship, a dressing table and so on. We did have three big flag poles at the corners that we could hang flags and things on at odd points but these didn't turn out to be all that useful. One, however, had a thick knotted climbing rope hung from it which we used for Scene 18 which all happens in mid-air.

Changing Scenery

The play must flow on smoothly without breaks except after Scene 13 THE BATTLEFIELD, though if you want to have more intervals there are other places they'll go. The actors coming on or going off can bring on or take off whatever's needed but have no gaps or pauses where nothing is happening unless it's a little bit of music or a sound effect.

Notes on the Scenes

Scene 1 SERMON needs a pulpit or box for the Vicar to stand on and perhaps a chair or box for Sir Gervase to sit on. A bit of organ music helps the church atmosphere at the start. 2 GERVASE AT HOME needs another chair or box for Bolt to sit on.

3 ON THE ROAD needs a clear stage. We used a skylark singing and in planning the journey imagined them walking from the moors above Whitby, where Peter Terson and I did the final rewriting of the play (in the Terson caravan), down to Portsmouth, bit by bit.

4 THE FIRST JOURNEY. All sorts of effects could add excitement to this. For the journeys the two or three actors walked on the spot while the rest sang the song around the stage. We dimmed the main lights down a bit and put the travellers in a spotlight. The music and the actors' walking movements really provide all you need though. For 5 THE GLUTTON a kind of dinner trolley crate was wheeled on by one servant while the other helped on the glutton and sat him on a chair. We had a sound effect of bees buzzing and wood pigeons cooing to make it seem like a very hot day. We made this the end of the meal so that we wouldn't have to provide a lot of food for the actor to eat, much to his disappointment. 6 THE HIGHWAYMAN needs an empty stage, dim light for night and perhaps a spooky owl effect. 7 ARREST used the empty stage and the soldiers marched their prisoners round it at the end while the actors brought on chairs and a bar for 8 THE CHAMP AND THE PRESS GANG.

Scene 9 ON THE ROAD AGAIN covered the removal of the bar and chairs and ended in an empty stage for 10 THE JOURNEY TO PORTSMOUTH. We ran some flags up the poles for 11 PORTSMOUTH BY THE ARMY CAMP and had a barrel of gunpowder on a low rostrum on castors. Two more of these were wheeled on to look like hatches and ropes were criss-crossed over the stage for 12 TROOPSHIP and we had a sea effect fading in and out during this. For 13 THE BATTLEFIELD the stage was cleared. Here the drummers and buglers were used to good effect and made fanfares at various points offstage till the last bit when they played a very loud fanfare to end Part One.

14 THE BATTLE was on an empty stage with the lights dimmed down for the dust storm. Sounds of cannon and other gunfire and battle sounds as well as the wind are needed in this scene. 15 JOURNEY ACROSS SPAIN was dimly lit with spotlights coming in here and there for different incidents. Sound effects for falling into bushes, into the river, for the shots and for jumping over the cliff are needed. The Mandalas possibly need some ferocious Spanish music. 16 THE FARM was done by lamplight and we used one of the rostra on castors for a kind of cart.

Scene 17 OUTSIDE SYLVETTE'S HOUSE was lit a bit more warmly and brightly — the first pleasant looking scene in Part Two, but with nothing on the stage except the knotted rope disguised as a creeper. Sir Gervase and Chunter climb up this rope for Scene 18 and are lit by a single spotlight some feet off th ground. While they are up there in Scene 19 Sylvette's dressing table and stool can be brought in and they descend to her level. It doesn't need a window — we certainly didn't use one. Here as in other places one part of the stage represents the balcony and another the room. They can be lit slightly differently. Of course, if you fancy it, most elaborate scenery could be used (or someone could make an exciting TV serial out of it, with real creepers and windows and battle-fields).

Scene 20 THE STREET was empty with a distant sound of crowds and gay music. 21 THE WEDDING could have an altar wheeled on. We had a deep tolling bell for the start. The altar was moved during Chunter's final speech. Scenes 22 THE GALLEY and 23 AT SEA used all our rostra stretched out to make a long ship and the slaves each had a long oar. Again sea effects are useful and possibly a rowing sound or a gong or drum to give the beat for the rowing strokes. The storm is a good place for the entire crew to rush off with the 'wreckage' of the galley except for one piece for Gervase and Chunter to lie or sit on for Scene 24 THE ENGLISH SHIP. For 25 THE GALLOWS a high plat-form was put together by the crowd and the soldiers and executioner and Sir Gervase needs to be up on this for his last speeches. There's no need for the rope to hang from anything — the executioner can just carry it around.

The stage is cleared for the last scene. The villagers need farm implements they can use as weapons. In the dance the idea is that they advance on Sir Gervase and Chunter raising their implements as if to strike them. But they form a circle close round them instead and give them each a tool to work with. Then they all dance together.

Cutting the Play

The script is very long, but Peter Terson and I decided we might as well let people read it all and cut out the bits they didn't like or didn't want to have in as they pleased, in order to make it shorter. It needs all the scenes and most of the incidents but each scene could be considerably shortened in a production.

Peter Cheeseman

(xii)

THE ADVENTURES OF GERVASE BECKET or The Man Who Changed Places was first presented at the Victoria Theatre, Stoke-on-Trent, on 18 March 1969 with the following cast:

CHUNTER	Arthur Whybrow
SIR GERVASE BECKET	Geoffrey Larder
VICAR	Alan David
GRIMTHORPE	Brian Young
NOBLEMAN BOLT	Christopher Whitehouse
BEGGAR	Christopher Martin
GLUTTON	John Keogh
HIGHWAYMAN	Ronald Forfar
SERGEANT	Alan David
OFFICER	Tim Hardy
INNKEEPER	Christopher Martin
CHAMP	Christopher Whitehouse
PRESS-GANG OFFICER	John Keogh
TOMMY TRIPLEFOOT	Brian Young
SERGEANT BROADWHISKERS	Ronald Forfar
FIERY GIRL	Gillian Brown
MANUEL	John Keogh
ENGLISH SOLDIER	Tim Hardy
FARM GIRL	Susan Glanville
SYLVETTE	Susan Tracy
PRIEST	Ronald Forfar
SYVLETTE'S FATHER	Brian Young
COUNT	Christopher Martin
ARAB CAPTAIN	Christopher Bond
BLIND LUMBA	Christopher Whitehouse
ENGLISH CAPTAIN	John Keogh
CRIMINAL	Christopher Martin
EXECUTIONER	Ronald Forfar
AMELIA	Gillian Brown
DOLLY TRIPLEFOOT	Carol Mason

Other parts played by members of the company. Autoharp played by Gillian Brown. Bugles played by Susan Glanville, Christopher Bond, Tim Hardy and Christopher Martin. Drums played by Brian Young and Christopher Whitehouse.

Directed by Peter Cheeseman
Costumes and setting by Anna Steiner
Fanfares music by Stuart Johnson
Journey music by Jeff Parton

Drawings by Peter Terson

Part One

BUGLE FANFARE. ENTER CHUNTER.

CHUNTER (AS NARRATOR): I'll tell you a story, cross my heart and hope to die if it ain't true about my master, who heard a sermon and took a journey, and was never the same man again.

ORGAN MUSIC. ENTER VICAR, PEASANTS AND GERVASE. GERVASE SITS IN FRONT OF PULPIT.

The sermon, I remember it well, because it was on the day of the village skittles final. The whole congregation was restless, except for my master whose two ears were laid out and flapping like the sails of a barque in the wind.

VICAR: And I say to my congregation —

Happy is the man who is content with his lot, contentment is great peace. Be ye free from the love of money and gain, being content with such things as ye have.

The man who is content with his lot will have fat sheep, plentiful milk from his cows and a house full of goodness.

But the man who is not content with his lot, he has a thorn in his side. He is never at peace, he is full of envy, he is made bitter by his envy. He covets his neighbour's goods and life. Let us not be vainglorious, envying one another, but let us be content with our lot.

And if you meet anyone who is dissatisfied, why then, change places.

AUTOHARP CHORD.

Give him your coat to wear, and take his rags, let him live in your house, and live in his house. Let him eat your food while you feed on his gruel. Give him your full purses, and go yourselves penniless. That is the challenge of the contented man.

ORGAN. PEASANTS AND VICAR FILE OUT. GERVASE IS MILES AWAY. CHUNTER SLEEPS.

CHUNTER: Oooh, where am I? In Church. Yes. Sir Gervase, Sir Gervase. He's miles away. Come back down to earth, Sir Gervase.

GERVASE: What did you think of that sermon, Chunter?

CHUNTER: It served its purpose. I slept from start to finish. I am just a fat contented fool, sir.

GERVASE: He is no fool who thinks himself a fat contented fool. I think I've been stirred. Stirred to my innermost soul.

CHUNTER: That must have been some sermon. When I woke you looked as though you couldn't be stirred with a bargepole. So far away you were. What was it about Sir Gervase? In a nutshell. Summing up. Quickly.

Here lies buried.
Grandad Gervase Becket

GERVASE: The man who is happy with his lot is blessed. Are you happy with your lot?

CHUNTER: There could be more of my lot. But otherwise I'm happy with it.

GERVASE: Are you happy to serve me?

CHUNTER: I'm contented squire Gervase.

GERVASE: Yes. I'm contented . . . I don't want to change . . . I have my land, I have you. I have my beasts; and you; I have my peasants and my woods, and you; I have my pheasants and my kind, and you; they all like life under me, I like life over them; why shouldn't it be like that?

CHUNTER: Let it stay like that. No need to change. Here comes the vicar, Sir Gervase, flying flat out like a magpie.

ENTER VICAR AT SPEED.

GERVASE: Sir, hold your flight.

VICAR: Sir Gervase?

GERVASE: Where are you flying off to like this? Errand of God is it?

VICAR: It's the village skittles finals today. I'm in the team. Skittling for a pig.

GERVASE: Well, let them skittle off, I want to talk to you today, do you know you skittled me with that sermon?

VICAR: I'm extremely delighted to hear it Sir Gervase.

GERVASE: If I asked YOU to change places today with somebody who wasn't in the skittle finals would you do it?

VICAR: I'd rather you asked me tomorrow, Sir Gervase.

GERVASE: On your way then. Go on. Skittle. Skedaddle.

VICAR GOES. THEY WALK HOME.

Look Chunter. Are you sure you're contented with your lot? Wouldn't you like to change? Don't you envy me?

CHUNTER: Envy you sir? Why should I? Look at the advantages of my life.

GERVASE: But if you were me. What are the disadvantages of that?

CHUNTER: Why, if I were you, and I were drinking in the beer house, getting all merry, my drinking pals would restrain themselves and murmur, 'That master's here'; it would be the same if I was up in the barn rolling in the hay with some plump wench . . .

GERVASE: You mean you do that?

CHUNTER: All the time sir. Except when I'm drinking. I'm the devil of the maids' lives. They love me though. So you see, I don't envy you your life.

GERVASE: Perhaps the vicar was wrong. Perhaps we should stick to our own lives. But I'm determined to find out. Go, and fetch Bailiff Grimthorpe, bring him to me.

CHUNTER: I'm as good as gone.

GERVASE: Have you been? Are you back yet?

CHUNTER: Sir. I'm not lightning.

GOES.

GERVASE: It's all so simple isn't it? If we were all contented, there'd be no envy in the world, if there was no envy no man would want other men's goods. There'd be no robberies, no wars, no hates. It would all be peace, and satisfaction. If envy were banished.

Scene 2 GERVASE AT HOME

ENTER CRIPPLED NOBLEMAN, BOLT.

BOLT: What's that? What's that? What you prattling about envy?

GERVASE: Forgive me sir, I've just been to Church.

BOLT: Bah to Church, don't give me Churches. That's where folk get married. I don't want Churches till it's time to get buried.

GERVASE: You're so unhappy sir. If I could change places with you.

BOLT: Never, never say that sir. Never say that. Listen, once upon a time I was a happy man, but I ENVIED. Now listen, I'll tell you. How's this for a tale. I was young, strong, a fencer of some ability, a boxer, a right old buck. I rode horses on Sundays, and gambled all Christmas night; I went after maid-servants, and flirted with nuns. I led a splendid life. However, one day, oy, what a day it was. I met this woman, of outstanding beauty. Beautiful, beyond all the world. And I loved her, and she had a host of admirers, we all loved her, and we surrounded her, BUT word got round . . . SHE WOULD NEVER MARRY.

GERVASE: This is incredible. Incredible. She would never marry? Why?

BOLT: BECAUSE SHE, under her skirts, had only one leg.

GERVASE: One leg?

BOLT: Actually she had two but one was made of wood. She would never marry a man with two legs. So, still stricken with love, I went to Paris, called a doctor into my hotel room, levelled a pistol at him and said, 'Take my leg off.'

GERVASE: Take it off?

BOLT: So the doctor hummed and hawed, but I threatened to shoot his brains out, and I would have done if he'd refused, so carried away as I was, by this love. And he amputated the leg.

GERVASE: Amputated it?

BOLT: Right off. Up to here. And me, happy as a pot-boy. Back to England, appeared before my love. Wooed her, and won her, she was so taken aback by my extreme measure.

GERVASE: You must have been a very happy man.

BOLT: Happy, hey ho, I was for a month or two. Then the novelty of the marriage soon wore off I can tell you. Sitting in every night, two legs between the two of us; no more fencing, no more boxing, riding, running, painting the town red. All I could do was sit in and sip brandy.

ERVASE: But the good lady, what about the good lady?

OLT: Good lady? She was a good lady. She could hobble about on her one leg like a cock robin, she was used to it you see. Hoh, but me, I never got used to it. I was lopsided. I could only drag myself about. She would rail at me for being a nuisance to her. Oh a right old tyrant. I'm going to a friend's house now to escape her; sit and drink brandy. He has gout, all my friends are crippled. I can't make friends with anybody else. Goodbye then. And don't exchange places with anybody. That's my advice. If you're happy, stick to it, and stay happy. That's my advice to you.

HE GOES. AUTOHARP. TENTATIVE CHORDS.

ERVASE: But I must. I must. If people are so unhappy I will change places with them. What right have I to be at ease?

ENTER CHUNTER WITH GRIMTHORPE.

A good day to you Grimthorpe.

RIMTHORPE: Is it? Is it a good day? If the peasants aren't sitting drinking ale, they're in Church; if they're not in Church they're playing skittles; if they're not playing skittles they're running with the wenches in the meadows . . .

HUNTER: Hah, what a life.

ERVASE: But it's Sunday, it's Sunday.

RIMTHORPE: They'll always find an excuse. Anything but work. The sun is shining, the hay is ready, the grass is green, the beasts want moved . . . oh I can't make headway.

ERVASE: Bailiff Grimthorpe, who do you envy?

RIMTHORPE: Envy? You. I envy you. A landowner.

AUTOHARP CHORDS.

OICE: Sir Gervase Becket. Step forward.

ERVASE: Would you change places?

RIMTHORPE: Like a clap.

ERVASE: Here then, wear my badge of office, my gown, my stick; take them, my house and grounds, they're all yours, and I promise I won't claim them back until I've reached the lowest of the low and changed places with the meanest slave.

HUNTER: Bravo.

ERVASE: If I meet a beggar, I'll change places with him.

HUNTER: Bravo.

ERVASE: If I meet the lowest, starving gypsy, I'll change places.

CHUNTER: That's my master.

GERVASE: If I have to I'll do so.

CHUNTER: To the end he will.

· GERVASE: I'm going on the road now Grimthorpe, or as you are now, Sir Grimthorpe, and I won't come back until I've suffered every hardship that anyone else has to bear.

CHUNTER: What a master.

GERVASE: And all I'll take with me is a bundle . . .

CHUNTER: Just a bundle.

GERVASE: And Chunter.

CHUNTER: He will that. What? Oh no sir. No. Sir, leave me here. I'm happy. Let me rot with the rest of mankind. I like it here sir, sir, I demand it. I respect it, I plead it, leave me here.

GERVASE: You don't want to come with me Chunter?

CHUNTER: As much as I love you sir. Never.

GERVASE: Then I'll go alone. Grimthorpe, it is all yours.

HE GOES. AUTOHARP CHORDS. GRIMTHORPE AND CHUNTER LEFT ALONE.

GRIMTHORPE: I'm master now. It's mine. I can do with it as I like. For years I've seen it managed in a lax manner. I've had to be bailiff of an inefficient, easy-going lot; now, I'm master, I can hardly believe it. Hi, Chunter, ring the bell, call the peasants . . .

CHUNTER: Oh, tart off Grimthorpe.

BELL RINGS.

GRIMTHORPE: Just stand over there while I address the peasants.

CHUNTER: Oh pouff to you Grimthorpe. I'm lost in thought.

GRIMTHORPE: Fat man, pick up that rake, and call me Sire.

CHUNTER: Sire? Me? You. Sire? And me the serving man of the squire? Pick up a rake? Me? For you? Sire? When I call you Sire, this place HAS changed hands.

THE NEXT BIT IS PUNCTUATED WITH CHUNTER'S 'SIRES'.

GRIMTHORPE (HITTING HIM WITH A STICK): Jump Chunter. (CHUNTER JUMPS.) Run Chunter. Sit Chunter. Stand Chunter. Pick up that rake Chunter, pick up that rake, right Chunter, now, get into the meadow Chunter, and get raking.

CHUNTER HAS BEEN GOING AT IT LIKE THE CLAPPERS.

They're creeping from their hovels and their ale houses and skittles. But I'm master now. I'll make them jump with a knotted rope end, I'll double them over till their backs are rounded, I'll have them working till their hands are blistering.

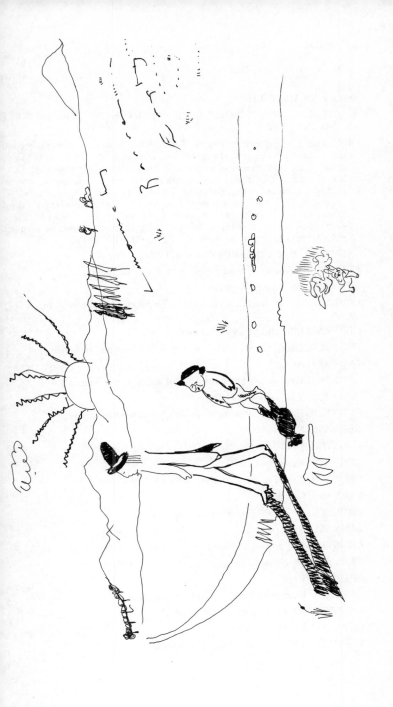

HE GOES. BELL FADES.

Scene 3 ON THE ROAD

A SKYLARK SINGS. JOURNEY MUSIC ON AUTOHARP. GERVASE WALKS
ALONG ON HIS TRAVELS.

GERVASE: I see my mission clearly. I must show the world that worldly goods
mean nothing. I am, as God made me; stripped of clothes all men are the
same. If any man envies me, let him take my place. I will rely on God; I'll
lead the simple life; if they strip me naked I will keep warm with . . . leaves.
If they deprive me of food I will feed on what the birds drop . . . berries
. . . and things . . . if I am thirsty and the ale house is barred to me, I'll drink
from what the animals drink . . . water. If the inn denies me a bed . . . I'll
sleep where the fieldmice sleep, in hay . . . I shall go so low that no man will
WANT to change places with me, but I'LL STILL BE HAPPY.

ENTER CHUNTER CARRYING SUITCASE.

CHUNTER: Sir Gervase, master, you've forgotten something.

GERVASE: What have I forgotten?

CHUNTER: Something fat, small, jolly, willing and eager to please. In a word,
me.

GERVASE: I thought you were staying.

CHUNTER: Have you ever made me jump with a knotted rope end?

GERVASE: Never.

CHUNTER: Have you doubled me over till my back was rounded?

GERVASE: You know I haven't.

CHUNTER: Have you made me work till my hands were blistered?

GERVASE: No.

CHUNTER: Did you ever intend to?

GERVASE: No. Never.

CHUNTER: Then I'm coming. Where's the carriage master?

GERVASE: Carriage?

CHUNTER: You always travel by carriage and four.

GERVASE: No carriage and four on this journey Chunter.

CHUNTER: Just horses? I'm game. Bit of canter adventure.

GERVASE: There are no horses on this journey, Chunter. Foot.

CHUNTER: Foot?

GERVASE: Foot. New travel method. Foot method.

CHUNTER: What about my luggage master?

GERVASE: Shoulder method.

CHUNTER: This makes the journey a toil master.

GERVASE: Possessions make life's journey a toil Chunter.

CHUNTER: That why you unladen master?

GERVASE: It is, Chunter. Off we go then.

CHUNTER SHOULDERS SUITCASE. THEY WALK.

CHUNTER: Master.

GERVASE: Brother?

CHUNTER: Master, I thought . . .

GERVASE: Call me brother.

CHUNTER: Sir Gervase . . .

GERVASE: Brother. From now on we are brothers.

CHUNTER: Sir Brother.

GERVASE: You will call me Brother, no titles, no fancy address. Brother. Or you may call me Gervase.

CHUNTER: Yeah. But if I call you Gervase, I'll feel that for my insolence I'll get a slap across the face. So, if I 'Gervase this', and 'Gervase that', I'll forever be twitching my ear out of range of your fist.

GERVASE: Have I ever hit you before?

CHUNTER: Have I ever called you 'Gervase' before?

GERVASE: Try it.

CHUNTER (TENTATIVELY): Gervase.

GERVASE (CALMLY): Yes brother.

CHUNTER: Gervase.

GERVASE: Yes Chunter.

CHUNTER: I find it very awkward calling you Gervase, Gervase.

GERVASE: You'll get used to it. My brother.

CHUNTER: This suitcase is heavy.

GERVASE: Possessions are a heavy burden.

CHUNTER: But I've just got the bare essentials in here.

GERVASE: Like what?

CHUNTER: Like . . . bare essentials . . . toothbrush, soap, flannel, blankets, plum cake, spare toothbrush, quilt. Beer. Folding mattress. Campbed. Bare essentials you see. I thought yours would be in the coach.

GERVASE: Chunter I travel as I am; the broken twig my toothbrush, the earth my mattress, the sky my blankets, the running stream my beer, the berries of the bush my plum cake. I need no suitcase.

ENTER BEGGAR. DRUM TAPS FOR HIS TROTTING PACE.

Well friend, you're moving on quickly. At a pace.

CHUNTER: He who travels lightest travels fastest.

BEGGAR: Hah, sir. That's true, but I wouldn't mind travelling slower but heavier. A few belongings is all I want in the world. I've never had belongings like . . . a few bare essentials, like a suitcase, wiv a . . . toothbrush, soap, flannel, blankets, bit of plum cake . . .

GERVASE (HINT): Many are those who have need. Blessed are those who would change places with those without. What lightens the back of one may gladden the heart of another.

CHUNTER HANDS OVER THE SUITCASE.

BEGGAR: Much obliged. (SCUTTLES OFF.)

BEGGAR TROTS OFF TO DRUM TAPS. SILENCE. THEY WALK.

Scene 4 THE FIRST JOURNEY

JOURNEY MUSIC. AUTOHARP. ACTORS AROUND LA AND WHISTLE.

CHUNTER (AS NARRATOR): We climbed up the long road, away from the village we knew and loved; up hill and down dale, across the moor and the bog to the world beyond, lying stretched out before us in a heat haze. (TO GERVASE.) Gervase.

THEY STOP. MUSIC STOPS.

My feet hurt. I have blisters, how far are we travelling?

GERVASE: Till sundown.

CHUNTER: But Gervase, this is the longest day of the year.

GERVASE: Then the longest marches will be over first.

MUSIC AGAIN. THEY WALK.

CHUNTER: We marched and marched, into the sun, out of the sun, I kept on, no complaining, but at last . . . I made a stand like the horse that had been driven to a standstill.

CHUNTER (TO GERVASE): Gervase. (STOP AGAIN.) For you I'd break my heart; but I'll not break my blisters.

GERVASE: Feet still hurt?

CHUNTER: Thirty miles ago it was agony, twenty miles ago it was unbearable, but now, it's immovable.

GERVASE: Chunter, nature provides at the wayside for the traveller's needs; the flower to glad his eye, the dock leaf to cool his blisters. Let me tend your feet.

CHUNTER: Master, in my suitcase there were bandages, ointments and brandy for blistered feet.

HE FIXES HIS FEET.

GERVASE: Then the beggar will be a happy man.

CHUNTER: He looked too leathery and worn to get blisters. So, on we went.

MUSIC. THEY WALK.

Whenever I flagged or my blisters cried out for rest, he would say —

GERVASE: Oh Chunter, when we rest we will rest like the Lords of Creation, we will dine like kings, eat like princes, drink like dukes.

CHUNTER: At last, I said — (TO GERVASE.) Master Gervase. (THEY STOP.) I'm hungry, when do we dine like kings, and eat like princes? Not to mention drinking like dukes?

GERVASE: Why, right now Chunter.

WOODPIGEONS COO. BEES BUZZ. THEY SIT ON THE GROUND IN A CORNER. A WOODED GLADE.

The world is our inn. We will dine like kings off blackberries and turnip; we will drink like dukes from this nearby stream.

CHUNTER: That's good to live off I must say. Blackberries and turnip; they don't agree with my stomach. I've brought some bread, would you like some bread?

GERVASE: If you'll share it with me brother.

Scene 5 THE GLUTTON

A WOODED GLADE. A FAT NOBLEMAN WADDLES ON WITH TWO SERVANTS DRESSED AS COOKS WHEELING A TROLLEY OF FOOD. GLUTTON SITS ON A STOOL AND IS FED. CHUNTER AND GERVASE LOOK ON. FIRST SERVANT BRINGS GRAPES TO GLUTTON.

FIRST SERVANT: Master, master, can you try another grape?

GLUTTON: Haaaa. Aaah. (EATS.)

SECOND SERVANT BRINGS CHOCOLATES.

SECOND SERVANT: A chocolate master? A chocolate?

GLUTTON: No. No. I'd die.

SECOND SERVANT: Soft-centred, master.

GLUTTON: Ugh, uhh. (EATS.)

FIRST SERVANT BRINGS BRANDY.

FIRST SERVANT: A sip of brandy master? Best quality?

GLUTTON: No. No. Never.

FIRST SERVANT: I'll serve it in drops till you've had enough.

GLUTTON: Uuuh, uhhn. (DRINKS.)

CHUNTER LOOKS AT HIS OLD CRUST.

GERVASE: It might look a little frugal Chunter, but look, to the bird in the sky, a crumb is a feast; a worm is a luxury, an insect is a dinner.

CHUNTER: I can't fly can I? My stomach is bigger than a bird's. My throat can swallow more than a sparrow's. I don't like worms. You speak nonsense.

GERVASE THROWS CRUMBS TO THE BIRDS. SECOND SERVANT BRINGS SWEETS TO GLUTTON.

SECOND SERVANT: Master, a Turkish delight. You know it's your favourite.

GLUTTON: Delight? Haaah.

SECOND SERVANT: I'll crumble it up ever so fine, and pop it in your mouth while you're asleep.

GLUTTON: Haaa. Haaah.

SECOND SERVANT DOES SO. GLUTTON EATS.

GERVASE: Was there ever such a pig? Such a hog? Was there ever a man like him. Hi there, was there ever such a greedy mammal as this? Has he any other organ but his belly?

FIRST SERVANT TIPTOES TO GERVASE AND CHUNTER.

CHUNTER: Mouth organ.

FIRST SERVANT: We servants think he must be all belly. He thinks food, lives food, sleeps food. When he goes on a journey of one day he takes with him a cart full of food, and a chef, and a kitchen staff.

CHUNTER: One day's journey. That's something.

GERVASE: What a giant eater.

FIRST SERVANT: That's nothing. When he goes to bed at night he has a table set all around him laden with food in case he wakes up for a snack.

CHUNTER: Can that be equalled.

FIRST SERVANT: You would think it couldn't. But listen. When he has a bath, he bathes in champagne in case he needs a sip.

GERVASE: The man's greed knows no boundaries.

FIRST SERVANT: Furthermore.

CHUNTER: There is more?

FIRST SERVANT: In his house, wherever he goes he has us servants making the sounds of food all the time, one will be squeezing oranges; another grating cheese, another milling flour, another cutting beef . . .

CHUNTER: Astonishment.

FIRST SERVANT: Same with sights, wherever he goes he has heaps of food; food is hung from the branches of trees that bear no fruit; his wells are full of milk; where other men keep pet dogs, he has pet goats and cows; other men have pictures of their ancestors on the wall; he has portraits of melons and apples and luxurious fruits of the East.

GERVASE: No more. No more. What a hog. He stirs.

FIRST SERVANT: He's getting ready for his coffee. Spiced in liqueur.

GERVASE: The man is a mountain of greed. It is unforgivable. He is one huge blancmange, a giant custard tart.

FIRST SERVANT: They say that if you prick him wine flows out.

CHUNTER: He stirs.

GLUTTON: Is the coffee ready?

FIRST SERVANT: I'll go for it my Lord, to the mobile kitchen. Cream?

GLUTTON: Don't tempt me. Yes. With cream.

FIRST SERVANT GOES. GLUTTON SEES GERVASE AND CHUNTER.

What are you after? My food? The crumbs? The remains? That's what you're after. There's a bird, after my scraps, away bird. Servant, pack this food away. We have a long journey ahead.

FIRST SERVANT COMES BACK WITH COFFEE.

FIRST SERVANT: Coffee my Lord. Do you want any brought to your friends my Lord? Cup of coffee for your friends?

GLUTTON: They're no friends of mine, they're beggars, scavengers. Look, they're begging for food. No. No coffee. We're short of coffee.

FIRST SERVANT: We've made half a gallon.

GLUTTON: We'll NEED THAT. Long journey ahead of us. Two miles to go. No. No coffee, stop asking for coffee you two.

GERVASE: We didn't ask for coffee.

FIRST SERVANT GOES.

We don't envy you your coffee.

CHUNTER: Or your food.

GERVASE: Or your fat.

CHUNTER: Steady on about fat. Don't be personal.

GERVASE: You have muscle. HE HAS FAT. Cream fat, cow fat.

CHUNTER: Grape fat, brandy fat.

GERVASE: Tit bit fat. You're fat and debauched. You have a paunch.

GLUTTON: Paunch?

GERVASE: Paunch. And let me see, one, two, three, four, five chins.

GLUTTON: Five?

CHUNTER: Who would own five chins.

GERVASE: You aren't even fit. We're fit. We can run round a tree.

THEY DO SO.

Do knees bend.

THEY DO SO.

Jump in the air.

THEY DO SO.

Stand on our hands.

CHUNTER CAN'T.

Well. I can.

GLUTTON (CRIES): Say no more, say no more. It's all right for you. Oh I envy you. I'd change places with you I can tell you. Listen I wasn't always like this. I could once do knees bend, jump in the air, nearly stand on my hands. I was fit, and young, and handsome, believe it or not, handsome. But I'll tell you what happened.

GERVASE: Tell us.

GLUTTON: When I was young, and handsome, I counted myself fortunate to marry the most wonderful angel on earth. How I loved that girl. But she was a flighty woman, hah, and unknown to me my young wife fancied my French chef, and he fancied her. And this French chef started to use all of his art and wiles to lure me to eat and become fat, and drowsy at night. And then they would go off together and sing under the moon and that sort of thing . . . this went on for weeks, years, and I grew into a thing so fat, and cumbersome that I noticed nothing . . . Then a trusty servant told me, I was furious, I was angry, I was beside myself. And they took fear and fled, and I chased them.

GERVASE: You were determined to get her back.

GLUTTON: No I was determined to get HIM back. I couldn't do without him. No food tasted the same without his cunning hand. I needed more and fresher tarts, novelties, new recipes to keep me satisfied. I fretted and wasted away . . .

CHUNTER: Without her?

GLUTTON: Without HIM you dolt, aren't you listening? At last I tracked them down and went on my knees, begging . . . for HIM to come back.

CHUNTER: And he came?

GLUTTON: Well, I promised him gold, freedom, power, I made him the second master in my own mansion, and he came back, he now lives like a Lord . . . in my house . . .

CHUNTER: And did SHE come back?

GLUTTON: No. She wasn't allowed back.

GERVASE: You wouldn't have her?

GLUTTON: He wouldn't have her. He was tired of her you see. So there was no alternative but for the two of us to ride back like reconciled lovers.

CHUNTER: You and her?

GLUTTON: Me and him.

GERVASE: And you've lived happily ever after?

GLUTTON: Not happy. I would willingly change places with you two.

   AUTOHARP CHORDS.

VOICE: Sir Gervase Becket. Step forward.

GERVASE: Change places.

GLUTTON: Yes. Seeing you reminds me of my youth when I was proud and sturdy, when I had friends, when I was fit and could walk on my hands. And it made me remember how that chef took my wife; and how if I had any pride I'd go back and beat him black and blue. Hah, if I could only change places with you how happy I would be. I'd soon get fit, and strong, independent.

GERVASE: Yes. You can. Look, if we change places. The two of us, with you and your servant. Send your mobile kitchen back to the mansion, and you go on foot to the place we've just left, and put yourselves into the hands of Bailiff Grimthorpe.

CHUNTER: Such tender hands.

GERVASE: And he'll give you the work we used to do . . .

GLUTTON: All right. Quick. Before I change my mind.

THEY ALL START TO STRIP. ENTER FIRST SERVANT.

FIRST SERVANT: Tea time — your chocolate eclairs my Lord.

CHUNTER GRABS FIRST SERVANT AND TAKES HIS CLOTHES.

CHUNTER: Thank you, they're ours, and your cloak is mine, and your hat is mine, and your jacket . . .

FIRST SERVANT: Master, I'm being stripped. I'm being unclothed. Laid bare.

GLUTTON: Do so, do so. Puff and pant, I didn't realize that taking off clothes was such hard and heavy work.

THEY ALL STRIP.

CHUNTER: Sir Gervase, brother, there's only one thing. The master's clothes fit the servant, and the servant's fit the master.

GERVASE: So be it. The master will wear the servant's robes and vice versa . . . you my man, are the master, and you will take your servant back to my estate, fifty miles walk down the road.

GLUTTON: FIFTY miles.

GERVASE: Go. And enrol with Bailiff Grimthorpe, and don't come back for a year. He'll give you a contract.

FIRST SERVANT: Right.

CHUNTER: And rounded shoulders, and cracked hands, and a broken back.

GERVASE: Here, take the switch. Make him move. Move there bullock.

CHUNTER GIVES HIM A SWITCH.

FIRST SERVANT: Move, fat pig.

GLUTTON: What. Why. Fifty miles? My horses aren't fit to walk that. Let alone me.

FIRST SERVANT: Move . . . (CUTS HIM WITH THE SWITCH.)

THEY CANTER OFF. HUNTING FANFARE.

Scene 6 THE HIGHWAYMAN

ENTER SECOND SERVANT.

GERVASE (TO SECOND SERVANT): Lead the way to your master's mansion.

SECOND SERVANT: Yes sir.

CHUNTER: And the custard pies with orange in, the brandy snaps and black-currant ice creams, the pigeons, and pheasant pies, the trifles, the long fizzy drinks, the strawberry puddings, the turkey rolls . . . lead on.

ENTER HIGHWAYMAN BEHIND THEM. MASK AND PISTOL.

HIGHWAYMAN: Stand and deliver.

CHUNTER: The egg flips, the sea food and melons, the oysters . . .

HIGHWAYMAN: Stand and deliver. I'll strip you naked.

CHUNTER: The shoulders of ham, the cheeses, the wines, the pears and oranges . . . oh, I knew it couldn't last.

GERVASE: You want our money friend? He wants our money Chunter.

CHUNTER: Oh, the first time I've had gold in my purse ever and he wants it . . . the custard pies, oh Lord, the custard pies.

HIGHWAYMAN: Empty it into this bag, and then sit, hands on heads.

GERVASE: Be consoled friend Chunter, be consoled. What good would it do us? If he wants it, then he must need it.

CHUNTER: The cream buns. The chocolate wafers, the lemon sherbet.

GERVASE: They might have given you indigestion.

CHUNTER: I've never had indigestion before. If that's the way you get it, I want it.

HIGHWAYMAN: Come on, stop the blather, I'm tough Dan, the highwayman.

CHUNTER: And I'm Chunter, that good food Hunter.

GERVASE: My plump friend. All this good living might have been bad for you. We were happy before we had all this finery.

HIGHWAYMAN: Is that so?

GERVASE: It is so.

HIGHWAYMAN: Then I'll have to take that finery and you can be happy again.

GERVASE: Then take it. Chunter and I were happy without these jewels.

HIGHWAYMAN: I'll have to take the jewels you know.

GERVASE: Then take them. Chunter and I were happy without fat purses.

HIGHWAYMAN: I'll have to take your fat purses.

GERVASE: Take 'em all. We're still happy.

HIGHWAYMAN: You're happy. I wish I was happy.

HIGHWAYMAN STARTS TO GO.

ERVASE: Why aren't you happy? You seem happy. You've got a mask, a horse.

HUNTER: Our jewels, big fat purses.

HIGHWAYMAN: I'm not happy. I'm sad. I must be the most miserable highwayman alive . . . once I was happy. I was an honest ploughboy. I used to sing behind the plough, 'Oh I am a jolly ploughboy who whistles o'er the lee . . .'

ERVASE: Never mind the overture, on with the story.

HIGHWAYMAN: Well I didn't mind the life, but I thought, 'How dull,' I want adventure. And so I packed up, and ran off. Now if the farmer had caught me I would have been beaten, so I ran fast, ah, but woe and alas I was young and impressionable and fell into bad company; I gambled, frequented ale houses, fell into severe debts until at last I was forced to steal, and then work on the highways.

HUNTER: Digging on them?

HIGHWAYMAN: Robbing on them. But now, my days are up.

ERVASE: How is that?

HIGHWAYMAN: For days now I have been pursued by the militia. I have been hounded and harassed; now, I am surrounded, the trap is about to be sprung and I am for the gallows.

ERVASE: Why do you hold us up? It won't do you any good at this late stage in the game.

HIGHWAYMAN: Hah, sir, this is my tragedy. I know no other way to live. I served my apprenticeship in crime and sin; now I wear them like my clothes. If only I could change places with a man of honour and decency I would make a fresh start.

AUTOHARP CHORDS.

VOICE: Sir Gervase Becket. Step forward.

ERVASE: Then highwayman, give me your clothes and rid of them, go your way with peace of mind.

HIGHWAYMAN AND GERVASE CHANGE CLOTHES.

There is a horse belonging to a glutton we have just met, take it, dash through the lines of infantry, go to my farm, and report to Bailiff Grimthorpe and start a clean life.

HUNTER: With a fresh slate.

HIGHWAYMAN: But I can't leave you to a highwayman's fate; when the soldiers come they tie you up, beat you about the head; then string you up on a gallows, hang you, draw you, quarter you; and then trail your body on the end of a rope through the streets . . .

HUNTER: Perhaps he's right.

ERVASE: No, this is my quest. You go or I'll have failed.

HIGHWAYMAN: Then I solemnly promise to go back to your Bailiff Grimthorpe, to obey him in all things; to do any work that I am given to do; in other words, to be grateful to you, and this opportunity to return to the farming life.

GERVASE: Then go, quickly. Without farewells.

HIGHWAYMAN GOES. HUNTING FANFARE. SILENCE. AN OWL HOOTS.

Scene 7 ARREST

CHUNTER: He's galloping off Master Gervase.

GERVASE: Is that his horse I hear in the distance?

CHUNTER: No, it's my knees knocking, they're going like a galloping mare.

GERVASE: What is it you're afraid of Chunter?

CHUNTER: The dark Gervase.

GERVASE: You're afraid of the dark?

CHUNTER: I'm afraid of robbers, and thieves, and cutthroats, and footpads, and highwaymen . . .

GERVASE: But that is us.

CHUNTER: Master, be reasonable. Why sit here waiting for the military? Throw away your highwayman's outfit into a ditch, ditch it; and assume your normal self.

GERVASE: Chunter I am wearing the garb, and the character of a highwayman and a villain, because I believe that goodness will shine through and win from the darkest, most hopeless situation on the earth . . .

A MILITARY DRUM IS HEARD GETTING NEARER.

CHUNTER: Oh, good; so you don't think we'll be whipped, beaten, hung till we're nearly dead? Drawn and quartered and our bits dragged through the streets . . .

GERVASE: I have faith Chunter. I have faith in the essential kindness and goodness of man.

CHUNTER: Gervase, in my experience, if you sleep with pigs, you smell like pigs in the morning; if you run with the foxes you get torn by the hounds; and if you consort with highwaymen and villains you end up hung drawn and quartered.

GERVASE: I cannot believe it.

ENTER POLITE SERGEANT AND SOLDIER.

SERGEANT: Excuse me, gentlemen, I must place you under arrest.

CHUNTER (SCREAMING): All right, do it now, get it over with.

SERGEANT: I beg your pardon sir?

CHUNTER: Beat me, smash me, hang me, draw me through the streets, but get it over with. I can't stand pain since I had my ingrown toe nail out.

SERGEANT: Would you step this way gentlemen? You're under my escort.

GERVASE: This is an awfully polite soldier.

HUNTER: He's biding his time. He's going to bring the flat edge of his sword on my back any minute. Go on.

SERGEANT: Gentlemen. You must come with me, we are quartered in a nearby inn.

HUNTER: Inn?

SERGEANT: Where you will be refreshed on bread and cheese and ale. A humble repast, but one fit for prisoners of the Army.

HUNTER: Bread and cheese and ale. Beat me first, then I'll enjoy it more.

SERGEANT: Prisoners ready to fall in. Escort stand by. (DRUM.) Gentlemen, with me please; all prisoners are considered innocent until proved guilty before twelve good men and true; you will be treated with all of the civility due to civilians of your rank. Gentlemen, step this way.

HUNTER: At the double?

SERGEANT: At your own pace.

HUNTER: With a rope's end?

SERGEANT: With courtesy. Forward march.

THEY MARCH. OFFICER BOUNDS IN.

OFFICER: Hah, got you. You're under arrest.

HUNTER: Well, we know that.

OFFICER: By God, that was a hunt. Caught you with my own hand. Well Sergeant, where have you been lurking? Stand up straight, they're my prisoners.

HUNTER: Your prisoners? We're HIS prisoners. We know who caught us.

OFFICER: Explain yourself Sergeant, where have you and the men been while I ran these prisoners to their liar?

GERVASE: He speaks like a fox hunting man.

SERGEANT: Well sir, since we last saw you, I took my men to search for the highwayman as were our orders; for seven days we have gone without sleep, searching every square yard of woodland; I then anticipated what you would have wished, scaled the cliffs, searched the caves; swam the river, in full pursuit. As we had no communication from you we slept out in the frost for two nights, got on his trail again, laid an ambush in the rain, heard him hold up some travellers and placed him under arrest.

OFFICER: But we started out in pursuit of only one. This one then is the accomplice?

HUNTER: Call me what you like sir.

OFFICER: Well, by jove, this is the most sensational capture I've ever made. This will give me promotion, I'll be ranked Major, I'll get a medal. I

pursued them to the ends of the earth, I'm made.

RGEANT: We're proud and pleased for you sir.

FICER: Drive 'em off.

RGEANT: Step this way gentlemen, please!

FICER: Give them a kick.

ene 8 THE CHAMP AND THE PRESS GANG

RUM CONTINUES. THEY MARCH ROUND. STOOLS AND BAR ARE
.OUGHT ON. UGLY CHAMP, GIRLS, INNKEEPER.

IUNTER (TO AUDIENCE): This man here. Oh, what a boaster, and what an
arrant knave. You've seen nothing for it. And what a coward. Yes, you'd
hardly believe it under that beautiful uniform, and swaggering air. But a
coward.

THEY STOP. CUSTOMERS DRINK.

Now in one corner of the inn was this man, squat, ugly. He had a hammered
face, as if it had been forged out of iron, rather badly chiselled by a poor
sculptor. It was an unfortunate face, but there was no need to MENTION it.

FICER: I have fought in campaigns in every part of Europe. Drinks all
round. Who won't drink with me? Stand up and drink with me. If you won't
drink with me, I'll drag you up. I have fought on horse, I have fought with
artillery; but this latest feat was a triumph, I cleared the King's Highway of
villains. Alone I did it. Give them a kick there. Is that ale they're drinking?

RGEANT: Quite cheap ale, sir. I bought it out of my own pay.

FICER: Kick it over. Throw it out in the backyard. I'll make them eat saw-
dust. Now where was I . . .

RGEANT (ASIDE TO GERVASE): I must apologize for this, prisoners.

FICER: Does anyone here want a fight? I'll fight anybody in this room.

NKEEPER: I'm sure sir, I'd keep a bit quiet if I were you.

FICER: If anyone in this room wants a fight, be it with fists, quarterstaffs,
r swords, I'm their man. If you won't frighten me, drink with me. Hi, some-
ne there doesn't drink with me.

RVASE: Who does he mean?

UNTER: That man with a face like a gargoyle.

FICER: Here, in a corner, snug,
        Sits a fellow with an ugly mug.

GIRLS SCREECH WITH LAUGHTER.

AMP: Please. Leave me be.

FICER: Here, in the corner, with his pint of porter,
        Sits an ugly man with a bashed in snorter.

AMP : Sir. Leave off.

OFFICER: What sort of man is this?

CHAMP: Please go way. Go way, please.

OFFICER: Are you a bird man?

CHAMP: No. Not bird man.

OFFICER: Then why do you speak Pigeon English?

GIRLS SCREECH AGAIN.

CHAMP: Please, away.

OFFICER: Don't brush me away my man, or I'll take a brush to you and sweep you about the ears with it. Will you fight?

CHAMP: No. Not fight. Leave be.

OFFICER: Then I'll make you fight. There, take that. Will you fight for honour

CHAMP: I don't fight for honour.

OFFICER: Then will you fight for anything?

CHAMP: Shall have to fight now. But I don't fight for honour.

OFFICER: What else is there to fight for? But honour? What else do you fight for?

CHAMP: Money. I'm the bare fist champion of the whole Middle of England. Make a ring, landlord.

TENSE DRUM BEATS.

INNKEEPER: Once he's decided to fight sir, nothing stops him. Make a ring, make a ring. He has fists harder than teak. The last man he hit he crushed his chin, terrible mess.

OFFICER (TO SERGEANT): Oh, what folly. Look I am in the uniform of my Regiment, proud of my honour and my career, now I fear it is all going to end

SERGEANT: End sir? With a fight of honour? Why should that end it sir? It doesn't matter if you are beaten, providing you are beaten honourably.

GERVASE: If I may add my endorsement of that sir. The honour of the Regiment is worth upholding. This is the point.

OFFICER: That is precisely not the point. Have you seen him? I would rather climb into a cage with a gorilla.

GERVASE: But for the sake of your Regiment.

OFFICER: I would change places sir, with any man who would wear that coat for me.

AUTOHARP CHORDS. DRUM STOPS.

VOICE: Sir Gervase Becket. Step forward.

CHUNTER (TO AUDIENCE): This could be the end of the story.

GERVASE: Sir, for the sake of your Regiment, let me take your coat.

OFFICER: Would you prisoner? If you would, I would let you both free. I would never be boastful again; I would leave the army, I would stop gambling, I would stop running off with women, I would trim my whiskers to a modest length. Will you take my place?

ERVASE: I will sir. Give me your coat, and go. One thing.

FFICER: Yes?

ERVASE: Go your way, and whatever happens, don't look back. Is that agreed?

FFICER: Sir, I will go so fast I won't be able to stop until I've covered ten miles. (HE GOES.)

HUNTER: What a coward.

ERVASE: But a repentant coward Chunter, there is nothing wrong with honest fear. So long as it is honest and not hidden by boasting. (HE PUTS ON THE COAT.)

INKEEPER: Ready to come out?

ERVASE: Ready.

INKEEPER: Do you want to take your coat off?

ERVASE: I want the whole world to know that my Regiment fought proudly. I'll keep my hat on.

DRUM. THEY START TO FIGHT. GERVASE GADS ABOUT, PEPPERS HIM. THE CHAMP JUST STANDS.

HUNTER: Use your reach Gervase. Pepper him. Use your left. Again. Use your footwork. Hit him hard. DANCE about Gervase, keep it moving in. Keep it going, you might last the distance and win on points.

BELL FOR THE END OF THE ROUND.

RVASE: He didn't fight. What's wrong? No man should be this shy. Perhaps he's wondering where to hit me. Look at my knuckles, all the skin off.

BELL AGAIN.

INKEEPER: Now, this time Champ. Go on, hit him. Aren't you going to fight Champ? What's wrong then Champ?

GIRLS SCREAM. INNKEEPER SHOUTS 'PRESS GANG.' ENTER TWO PRESSMEN. ALL FLEE. PRESSMEN TRY TO TAKE THE CHAMP BUT HE KNOCKS THEM ALL OVER THE PLACE.

RVASE: Well, Chunter, how do you fancy the Navy?

UNTER: I don't.

RVASE: It looks as though we'll soon be jolly tars. If you don't submit they hit you with their rope's end.

UNTER: Submit. Look at the champ. I thought he couldn't fight.

PRESSMEN GO TO GERVASE AND CHUNTER.

UNTER: All right shipmate, we're ready. Hearts of Oaks are our Ships.

ENTER PRESS OFFICER.

PRESS-GANG OFFICER: Leave him sailor. Can't you see he's an officer of the British Army?

HUNTER: I'm his batman. My uniform's at the laundry.

PRESS-GANG OFFICER: Beg your pardon Lieutenant.

GERVASE: Not at all brother of the Navy.

PRESS-GANG OFFICER: Drink sometime?

GERVASE: Let's.

PRESS-GANG OFFICER: Good job you were in uniform, they'll take anything on two legs. Right, must get on. 'LEAVE HIM ALONE THERE. You'll never arrest him. Get the others.'

THEY GO, LEAVING CHAMP, GERVASE AND CHUNTER.

GERVASE: Well Champ, you saw them off. Want to finish our fight?

CHAMP You don't want to, do you?

GERVASE: Why not? I was doing all right.

CHAMP: Oh, I could have killed you my old friend.

GERVASE: Why didn't you then?

CHAMP: Because I had a bet of a hundred pounds on that you would last three rounds. In the third round I was going to give you ONE hit, one hit — (HE DEMONSTRATES.) to put you out of your misery.

GERVASE: Thanks friend.

CHAMP: But now. Peace. Brother, I admire your courage, taking that coward's place. (HE HUGS HIM.)

GERVASE: Help, help. Oh my God, if that's his love, thank goodness I didn't get his hate.

CHAMP: Shake hands.

GERVASE: No. Not with that grip. Let's kiss.

PAUSE. CHAMP BOWLS HIM OVER WITH A FRIENDLY SHOVE AND GOES OFF. ENTER CAVALRY OFFICER EXCITED.

OFFICER: I could have killed him.

GERVASE: You said you wouldn't look back.

OFFICER: Pooh to that. You didn't think I was serious did you? Of course I looked back.

GERVASE: You have no honour sir.

OFFICER: Are you looking for a fight?

GERVASE: I've just found a fight that I didn't look for.

OFFICER: I could have killed him. He was like a flat-footed old bear. He didn't move. I would have danced around him like you did, only stronger, I have a good punch. I would have worn him down and then when he was exhausted, beaten him to pulp.

GERVASE: Sir, you're a disgrace to your Regiment.

OFFICER: Oh, pooh to that. I would have murdered him. I'll tell the fellows in the barracks when I get back, what a flat-footed old ham the champion of the Midlands was.

GERVASE: You shan't wear this uniform again.

OFFICER: Pooh to that. I shall buy a new one. I wouldn't put it on after you've sweated in it.

ENTER PRESSMEN. GIRLS SCREAM AGAIN.

CHUNTER: Pressgang.

OFFICER: They can't touch me. I'm Officer class.

PRESS-GANG OFFICER: You'll do. Get him.

OFFICER: I'm an acting Major.

PRESS-GANG OFFICER: We'll see how you do for a real seaman.

OFFICER: But look, I'm horse. I have my sword and uniform. (REALIZES HE HASN'T.) Sergeant! Tell them.

PRESS-GANG OFFICER (TO GERVASE): Excuse us brother Officer.

SERGEANT: My Regiment cannot help civilians.

CHUNTER: He's a rowdy person, I think you'll have to put him to sleep.

PRESS-GANG OFFICER: Put him to sleep.

THEY CLUB THE CAVALRY OFFICER WITH THEIR ROPES AND CARRY HIM OFF.

Good day to you brother Officer.

PRESSMEN GO.

Scene 9 ON THE ROAD AGAIN

CHUNTER: Let's keep away from Portsmouth shall we? If they're pressing for men in the heart of England what must they be doing in seaports.

GERVASE: We have no choice in the matter. The Sergeant will escort us to the Court Martial.

SERGEANT: There will be no Court Martial for you sir.

GERVASE: No Court Martial? But I am your prisoner.

SERGEANT: Sir, my Officer ordered me to catch you; and I caught you. He has now given orders to release you, so I release you.

CHUNTER: We're free! I can't believe it. Sounds of war all round, Armies in one direction, highwaymen in the other, Navies with tarred ropes and we've missed the lot of 'em.

GERVASE: Well Sergeant, whither are you bound?

SERGEANT: As your companion said, the sounds of war are all round, and I have to march south to Portsmouth. Will you accompany me part of the way

I should be honoured and delighted at such company.

ERVASE: Honoured here also.

HUNTER: And here.

ERVASE: But this Officer's uniform, and no Officer to wear it. Can I grant you my new won commission? It is customary to buy a commission; I would like to give it away.

RGEANT: Sir, I am a man of noble birth. My father was wealthy, and influential, he gave my elder brother and I everything; we neither had to fight, nor to struggle. Through having life too easy my brother became lax, and dissolute and spoiled his character. I decided that the only school was the school of life and resolved that everything I gained in life would be worked for. Thus, I signed on in the Army as a mere private and wish to work for every step of progress.

ERVASE: Chunter, we have another philosopher here. Well, Sergeant, lead on.

THEY WALK. JOURNEY MUSIC.

ene 10 THE JOURNEY TO PORTSMOUTH

HUNTER (AS NARRATOR): Philosophy is all very well, but since Gervase took up philosophy I seem to have taken up walking. We walked through Staffordshire, and they talked philosophy.

THEY STOP. MUSIC STOPS.

ERVASE: Plato said that the perfect citizen should abide by the Rules of the Ideal Republic.

RGEANT: Socrates said that the citizen should face death if the country's law demands it.

HUNTER: My belly says it's tea time and he's a philosopher who's never wrong.

ERVASE: Aristotle, he said . . .

THEY WALK AGAIN. MUSIC.

HUNTER: Through Worcestershire and Gloucestershire they talked Literature.

THEY STOP. MUSIC STOPS.

ERVASE: Shakespeare sat for forty days and nights to write Act One of *A Midsummer Night's Dream.*

RGEANT: Bunyan sat in a cell to write *Pilgrim's Progress.*

HUNTER: My bum hasn't sat down for a fortnight. And words can't describe it.

THEY WALK. MUSIC.

Through Wiltshire and Hampshire it was music . . .

ERVASE: The measures of Bach are suited to the contemplative man.

RGEANT: And the rhythms of Scarlatti are for the dancer.

CHUNTER: My feet are built for a sitting down man.

GERVASE: Handel was a composer of considerable powers . . .

CHUNTER: I would have been happier if the Sergeant had told Gervase that the best philosophy was sitting at home by the fireside with a pot of ale and a wench. But no such luck; we reached the parting of the ways and took our farewells.

MILITARY DRUMMING AND FANFARE.

GERVASE: Well farewell courteous Sergeant, and may fate be kind to you.

SERGEANT: And my friend, a word of advice, don't look for trouble.

GERVASE: We don't look for trouble; and if all men were as content with their own lot as you are then we could give up our mission and go home.

CHUNTER: Home! The wisest word spoken yet.

SERGEANT: If you should ever need my help and I was available I would be glad to rush to your assistance.

GERVASE: The world is wide, the world is large, but the world is round and we may come face to face again.

CHUNTER: Cripes, is he thinking of going round the world then?

GERVASE AND SERGEANT EMBRACE. SERGEANT GOES.

Scene 11 PORTSMOUTH BY THE ARMY CAMP

BY THE ARMY CAMP. FLAGS. A BARREL OF GUNPOWDER.

CHUNTER: Well, we got rid of the Sergeant and in a way I wasn't sorry to be away from the Military. It makes me uncomfortable, I don't want to be caught up in their cannons, their wars, and battles; I was about to suggest that we should turn right and nip down to Cornwall, which always strikes m as a peaceloving land . . . when . . . horrors . . .

GERVASE: Listen, the sounds of distress.

CHUNTER: Oh blimey I know what that means. When there's a bit of distress. In we step. Both feet. Feet first. Plop.

ENTER SOLDIER AND WIFE WITH BABY.

GERVASE: You look in trouble friend. Can we help you?

SOLDIER: No one can help us sir.

CHUNTER: That is the best news this week.

GERVASE: Then what is your trouble?

SOLDIER: It's so sad sir, that it hurts me to repeat it.

CHUNTER: That's a good argument, it would hurt me to listen.

GERVASE: Tell us all the same, the telling may relieve your heart a little.

CHUNTER: And burden ours.

SOLDIER: If you wish to hear the most miserable story alive sir, then prepare to shed tears. It was like this. To cut a long story short, as a boy I was forced by my stepfather to join the Army against my will.

GERVASE: How unfortunate.

SOLDIER: However, in one thing, I was fortunate. I met and made my own, this dear woman.

CHUNTER: Pleased to meet you ma'am.

SOLDIER: We travelled around the country, always keeping together and had this lovely child. However, tomorrow the Army is going abroad.

GERVASE: And you're going with them?

SOLDIER: Yes.

GERVASE: Can't you take your wife with you?

SOLDIER: Yes. The soldiers drew lots to decide who should take their wives and we won one of the places.

GERVASE: Why, then things might turn out for the better.

SOLDIER: Have you been on a troopship sir?

GERVASE: I haven't had that experience. No.

SOLDIER: They herd the men down below like pigs; never seeing the light, they whip you, throw swill down at you, men are seasick over each other till the place is running in foul smelling things.

GERVASE: That's unpleasant. But you'll survive. The human spirit is strong.

SOLDIER: Then, after a week of no fresh greens, the scurvy starts. Your skin dries up, and you cry for a bite of lettuce, or a piece of cabbage. Men fight each other to the death for fresh greenstuffs.

GERVASE: I'd hate that life. How like animals men can become.

WIFE: The only hope a mother has of keeping her baby is to tie it to her, or surely it will be snatched away from her by the sailors, or lost overboard in the storms.

CHUNTER: This is infamous.

GERVASE: But you WILL reach land friend, be comforted, you will reach land.

SOLDIER: But have you seen a foreign battlefield sir? It is no place for a dog, let alone a woman and a baby.

CHUNTER: I can imagine that.

SOLDIER: Following the Army; with all the disease, and death, and blood and dirt . . .

WIFE: And if he is killed, as is likely, it will be a mercy if he has a quick death; more probably he will linger on in the battlefield; with his body rotting of some musket ball; or his head cut with a sabre, trodden into the mud . . . dying . . . limbless . . .

CHUNTER: Don't, I can't bear blood.

WIFE: If he dies, I am left in a foreign battlefield, alone . . .

CHUNTER: Actually, we've got to be off now.

WIFE: Oh we are lost. Lost. I am in despair for myself and the child.

SOLDIER: There, settle down dear; oh sir, if only I could change places with you.

CHUNTER: Oh my Gawd, he's said the magic words. Here we go. We're off again.

AUTOHARP CHORDS.

VOICE: Sir Gervase Becket. Step forward.

GERVASE: Would you change places with us soldier?

SOLDIER: But how is it possible?

GERVASE: Suppose we made it possible?

SOLDIER: Don't torment us sir. Leave us in our misery.

GERVASE: But if we made it possible?

SOLDIER: Then there is nothing I would like more dearly.

GERVASE: Well, look here, I have a map, and this map shows you the way to a farm, and manor house where you will be welcomed by a man named Grimthorpe.

CHUNTER: Just a minute, just a minute, hold your horses.

GERVASE: There you and your wife can stay until my return. When that will be, no one knows, but you will be given a shelter, roof over your head, a little garden.

WIFE: Oh sir!

CHUNTER: Just a minute, just a minute, whoaaa . . . hold on.

SOLDIER: Can we do it?

GERVASE: What do you say to it?

SOLDIER: Sir. I can never forget this.

CHUNTER: Just a minute, just a minute, just a minute.

GERVASE: What are you 'just a minuting' about?

CHUNTER: It can't be done.

WIFE: Haaah, sir, it was cruel to boost our hopes up like this.

GERVASE: It will be done.

CHUNTER: Cannot be done, absolutely not feasible. Absolutely imposs.

GERVASE: It will be done. If this man and his wife go now.

CHUNTER: But WHO takes his place in the Army?

GERVASE: I do. I shall wear his uniform.

CHUNTER: Hah, yes, easily enough. But who takes the place of his good wife?

GERVASE: May I take your bonnet madam?

WIFE: Yes. Here.

GERVASE (PLANTING IT ON CHUNTER'S HEAD): You are the wife.

CHUNTER: Oh Gawd, help us. No. I don't want to be a wife.

GERVASE: You must be a wife. Now, madam, if you would go and conceal yourself, Chunter will throw you his clothes, and your husband and I will change clothes here.

CHUNTER: Aw, I don't want to be a wife, I tell you.

GERVASE: Quickly. Now, get changed.

FANFARE. GERVASE AND SOLDIER CHANGE UNIFORMS. CHUNTER GOES OFF WITH WIFE.

GERVASE: When we are ready you and your wife must take to the road quickly, follow that map; you'll travel better dressed as two men. One thing, you MUST promise to work for Grimthorpe.

SOLDIER: Sir, I'd serve anyone to keep my wife with me.

GERVASE: Good, and when I return you can do as you wish; come or go.

SOLDIER: To whom do I owe my freedom sir?

GERVASE: To whom? Why, to me, Gervase Becket, the man who changed places.

SOLDIER: You're my Saviour then sir, and let anyone tell Tommy Triplefoot that Gervase Becket is not the best man alive and I'll deal with him with his stick.

GERVASE: Hah, here's your wife. You must go immediately.

ENTER CHUNTER AND WIFE.

SOLDIER: You're as lovely as ever.

GERVASE: And good wife, you're as lovely as ever. Embraceable and lovable.

CHUNTER: Is that it? Well I'll be a scold I can tell you. I'll make your life a misery. I'll give you my tongue from morning till night. I'll get at you in your sleep. I'll make a change-places man of you.

GERVASE: Quickly, now you must go.

SOLDIER: Then, goodbye and God bless you.

WIFE: And from me and the child. God bless you both.

THEY GO. FANFARE.

CHUNTER: God bless us both? Yes, the same God who made us man and wife. What a Union this is.

GERVASE: Wasn't it worth it to have their gratitude?

CHUNTER: Worth it. Oh don't speak too soon. You don't speak too soon. Worth it. We'll see if you are of the same mind when I've made your life a misery.

GERVASE: Is there any need to be such a scold.

CHUNTER: Any need? I'll say there's need. Need? You want me to act the wife. All right, I'll act the only sort of wife I know. All the wives I know are nag wives. So get moving. Find me straw for a bed, and build a fire; we'll use the soldier's Billy can as a kettle. I want a hot drink. Hurry, jump to it. Go on.

GERVASE: Certainly my dear. Yes my dear. (HE GOES.)

CHUNTER: Have you ever seen anything like it? What are men coming to? They don't wait on a girl any more. Just think they can dawdle and hang about. What did I marry him for? Decoration. (SHOUTS.) Go on, get searching, I want my comforts.

SERGEANT BROADWHISKERS BEHIND THE BARREL WITH A CURLY MOUSTACHE.

BROADWHISKERS: What a spirit, what a woman. I love a woman with a bit of body and spirit to her.

CHUNTER: And another thing, we'll see who wears the skirts in this house. The times in our lives that you've been master, but no more.

BROADWHISKERS: He used to be master eh? But she's changed all that.

CHUNTER: There'll be no more 'sirs,' and 'your honour' from me.

BROADWHISKERS: Oh, that's telling him. Quite right, quite right. Only a milksop woman respects her husband. Psst. Psst.

CHUNTER: I'll psst, psst you. What you pssting at?

BROADWHISKERS: Psst, psst. Here.

CHUNTER: And none of your tricks. Go on, on with your work. That's funny, he went that way and now he's pssting from behind.

BROADWHISKERS: Psst. Psst. I'm a Sergeant.

CHUNTER: That was quck promotion. Haaah.

BROADWHISKERS: Hello my duck. Is your big fury over yet? You can set up a fine cackle. You did didn't you?

CHUNTER: Oh I did. A fine old cackle.

BROADWHISKERS: I like a woman who is a duck.

CHUNTER: He doesn't realize he's got a drake.

BROADWHISKERS: What's your name darling?

CHUNTER: That's funny. What is it? My married name? I'm afraid it's not worth remembering.

BROADWHISKERS: Ho, what a woman. Not worth remembering your married name eh? That's good. And true, and true, they're not worth a fig married names aren't. Nor husbands.

CHUNTER: You better be careful. Here is my husband.

ENTER GERVASE WITH STRAW.

BROADWHISKERS: Hah, private. Up straight when I speak to you. Up, up like a ramrod, or I'll break you.

CHUNTER: Get him any straighter and you'll snap him.

BROADWHISKERS: Oh, you bird. Now, private, not a ribbon eh? Not a medal, you're as green as new shoot grass, what's your wife's name?

GERVASE: Why do you want to know it?

BROADWHISKERS: Sergeant. Sergeant. Why do you want to know it Sergeant. I want to know it because I have declared my interest to know it. Now, your wife's name.

GERVASE: I am under no obligation to divulge my wife's name.

BROADWHISKERS: Then YOUR name clever stick. YOUR name.

GERVASE: But by that devious method you will get at my wife's name.

BROADWHISKERS: Give me your name, or I shall bust you.

GERVASE: You may break my bones, never my spirit or honour.

BROADWHISKERS: I can break you, your health, your name, your spirit, your honour, unless you tell me your name.

GERVASE: What can you do if I refuse?

BROADWHISKERS: I can order you to be whipped round the battalion with a cat of nine tails.

GERVASE: Can you order that?

BROADWHISKERS: I can. And then have vinegar and salt rubbed in the wounds.

CHUNTER: You have the legal right to do that to a man who withholds his name?

BROADWHISKERS: I have.

CHUNTER: His name's Tommy Triplefoot, and I'm his wife, Dolly.

BROADWHISKERS: Dolly Triplefoot, that's a wonderful name. And are you light of foot Dolly Triplefoot, and will you trip with me the light fantastic on your triplefoot?

CHUNTER: We'll dance ere long Sergeant.

BROADWHISKERS (DOES A FEW TWIRLS): Till then my Dolly Triplefoot. I'll see you under the moon, on board the ship . . .

CHUNTER: Ship?

BROADWHISKERS: That takes us to the battlefields of Spain.

GERVASE: But in all that mud, and grime, and filth, and blood.

BROADWHISKERS: Look, we're going to Spain, there'll be no grime, and mud and filth, just blood.

GERVASE: Blood?

BROADWHISKERS: Thine. Not mine.

GERVASE: Mine?

BROADWHISKERS: Yes. But I'll comfort her, and let her tears flow till they are a flood, and they'll wash away the blood.

GERVASE: This is a gory story.

BROADWHISKERS: I don't let a chance like this slip. I'll see you on board the troopship, farewell Dolly Triplefoot. Ask for Sergeant Broadwhiskers, of the Fourteenth Foot.

HE GOES. SHIP'S WHISTLES.

Scene 12 TROOPSHIP

ROPES AND HATCH TOPS BROUGHT ON. SEA NOISES.

CHUNTER (TO AUDIENCE): Within hours we were on board ship and set sail. Sailors dashing up the rigging, much coming and going, whistles and pipes; and there we were. We girls were all huddled up together in the front part of the deck. Wives of the soldiers. There was this fiery girl beside me. Hoh, if only I could have thrown off my women's garments, what a time I would have had.

WOMEN CROWD AROUND.

I say.

GIRL: What do you want?

CHUNTER: You look miserable.

GIRL: I am miserable. Who wouldn't be miserable thrown about here, like cattle. Having to listen to the wailing and caterwauling of the wives.

CHUNTER: But you're with your husband.

GIRL: I am not with my husband. I had a young Lieutenant, he persuaded me to come with him. He looked a grand lad on land; in his scarlet uniform, dancing and tripping about; and I'd never had an Officer before, so I arranged to come with him. But, lo and behold, he doesn't travel on the same ship as me. No, he's on the Admiral's flagship, drinking wine in the Captain's cabin. While I won't have water to drink. Here's the type of man I'll have. I won't have Officers any more.

ENTER BROADWHISKERS.

BROADWHISKERS (TO CHUNTER): My duck.

GIRL: What does he see in her? She's fat and lumpy; well, I'm not fat and lumpy, only in the right places where a girl should be fat and lumpy.

BROADWHISKERS: My Dolly Triplefoot. I've been trying to find you, I've been on duty, bullying the soldiers into cleaning the brasses. Sharpening their bayonets, and preparing their rifles.

CHUNTER: Where are the soldiers?

BROADWHISKERS: They're in the hold, down there, five hundred of 'em. With the rats and the cockroaches they are. Living on ship's biscuits with weevils in them. Some of them sleep up to their necks in bilge water, and others have to lie on the hard timbers of the ship. It is a laugh.

GIRL: She's such a stupid lump. She has a voice like a foghorn, or a man; and why does she hide her hair under that ridiculous bonnet? Look at her skin, I could swear she needs a shave, and those feet and hands, what a pair of maulers for a girl to have. Look at my feet and hands.

CHUNTER: What have you done with my Tommy Triplefoot. Have you given him special treatment?

BROADWHISKERS: Oh very special for him. At the stern end of the ship where it points, there is a little part there where most of the bilge water gathers; the timbers there are covered with seaweed, and green moss; and when the ship rolls and rises, it rolls and rises there the most, and when the food is passed down the hatch, by the time it reaches him there's none left; and when anyone is seasick . . .

CHUNTER: He gets it?

BROADWHISKERS: Yeah, and he gets no air, no light, nor warmth. He seems to be enjoying it down there though. When I creep down, over the murk and filth, putting my boot into some retching soul and say to him, 'How are you Tommy Triplefoot?' he replies, 'I am well Sergeant. How good of you to come and ask. Man is all goodness that he will come and care for his fellows, at the risk of getting his clean boots covered in slime and sickness. Thank you Sergeant, you're most kind, and courteous and God is best to those who have least.' Is he a maniac? Was he from a home before the Army?

CHUNTER: He was from a home. A good home. The best there was bless him.

BROADWHISKERS: He was even taking the beetles out of his biscuits, and putting them in a little box with bits of his own whiskers to keep them warm.

CHUNTER: WHAT a saint.

BROADWHISKERS: Give us a kiss Dolly Triplefoot.

CHUNTER: With that wax whisker; I'll be speared.

WOMEN SHRIEK.

BROADWHISKERS: Come on duckling.

CHUNTER: No. Not on deck.

BROADWHISKERS: I'm pleading.

GIRL: Go on, give him a kiss. Go on, some have all the luck. Stop being coy you old heifer, what's wrong with you woman, give him a kiss, I'm warning you, if you don't, I shall. And there'll be no mistake.

GOES TO GIVE BROADWHISKERS A KISS. THE GIRL SHOVES CHUNTER OUT OF THE WAY AND THEY BEGIN TO FIGHT.

CHUNTER: Here, leave me alone. Don't scratch me. Hi, you need your nails cut. Don't tear at me. Watch my bonnet.

BROADWHISKERS: Go on Dolly, give her something. Start up DOLLY.

HE TRIES TO INTERFERE. CHUNTER PUNCHES HIM TO THE GROUND.

CHUNTER: I don't hit ladies.

GIRL PULLS HIS BONNET OFF.

BROADWHISKERS: So this is it.

CHUNTER: Oh Lordie.

WOMEN SHRIEK.

BROADWHISKERS: So what's your game?

CHUNTER: Give us a kiss, missus.

BROADWHISKERS: Make a fool of me would you? All right. All right, I know
how to deal with you. To the bilge water with your husband. I'll marry you
to death. When we get to the Peninsula I'll put you in the thick of battle,
where explosives and shot parches your throat, where water is scarce but
blood is in flood, I'll send you charging into a pack of bristling bayonets that
makes a hedgehog look naked. I'll put you in front of the cannon's mouth
that has more teeth than an alligator; I'll put you on foot to face the charges
of horses, that sounds like thunder . . . I'll, I'll . . . GET DOWN TO THE
BILGE WATER.

CHUNTER DASHES OFF.

GIRL (TO BROADWHISKERS): I love kind men sweetie. Give us a kiss!

THEY EMBRACE.

Scene 13 THE BATTLEFIELD

BROADWHISKERS (TO AUDIENCE): So I decided to put them in the thick of
it. When we got to Spain, all the tackles was hauled down, the sailors dashed
up the rigging and stowed the sails; and we disembarked with our horses and
provisions and weapons and I PUT THEM IN THE THICK OF IT . . . no hard
feelings of course.

DRUM. GERVASE AND CHUNTER MARCH ON WITH RIFLES.

Right, Tommy Triplefoot and wife; you take up your positions here. Over
there is the enemy; infantry. (BUGLE CALL.) They will pepper you con-
stantly with shot.

GERVASE: Shot?

BROADWHISKERS: Little lead pellets, torn wire, musket ball; nothing lethal,
just pepper you to bits. (DRUM.) Now, down that hill there the cavalry will
charge you, about five hundred of them, the ground is firm so they'll be
travelling at full speed here, waving their cutlasses and lances, as if they were
sticking pigs.

CHUNTER: They might think we're not worth the sport.

BROADWHISKERS: Over there is a swamp, if you last till midday the fever
flies will be all over you, sun gets hot here. Behind, is the Russian Cannon,
they'll be erasing all within a square mile of this position.

GERVASE LOOKS IN THE ONLY DIRECTION LEFT.

GERVASE: What about up there? That looks clear.

BROADWHISKERS: That's where the worst enemy is. That's the enemy you've got to fear most. He's mad, wild, he goes berserk, he tramples, gnashes his teeth, he is a wild man in battle. Me. Now here's your flag, lose it, and you're hung drawn and quartered. See you.

CHUNTER: When?

BROADWHISKERS: In heaven or in Hell.

EXIT BROADWHISKERS. DRUMS. CHUNTER AND GERVASE STAND BACK TO BACK. MIGHTY MENACING FANFARE.

END OF PART ONE

Part Two

Scene 14 THE BATTLE

GERVASE AND CHUNTER, BACK TO BACK, WITH GUNS. FUNERAL-SOUNDING FANFARE. DRUM BEAT.

GERVASE: Why are we in front of everybody else?

CHUNTER: I wouldn't have minded, I don't think, if . . .

GERVASE: Those back there think they're in the thick of it; and those forward there think they're in the thick of it, but US, we're between the two of them in no man's land.

CHUNTER: I don't think I'd have minded, like, if . . .

GERVASE: You what?

CHUNTER: I wouldn't have minded this . . . these guns. If he'd shown us how to load them.

GERVASE: It is a grave disadvantage . . . (DISTANT CHARGE SOUNDED.) Well, Chunter. It looks as if we're at the end of the road. My only regret is . . . that I had to bring you to this.

CHUNTER: That's my only regret too.

GERVASE: The only thing a man can take to heaven, is himself.

CHUNTER: And his servant.

GERVASE: But we have thrown down the barriers of class, of master and servant, and become, brothers.

CHUNTER: Dead brothers.

CANNON BOMBARDMENT BEGINS.

GERVASE: Farewell then. Stand firm my brother; set your sights on the enemy and your eyes to heaven.

CHUNTER: Where do I point it? Who are we fighting?

GERVASE: We're fighting in Spain, against the Spanish; and the French, so the North Germans are helping us and they have some Russians helping them, and some South Germans from Schlesvig Holstein. You'll also notice some brightly clad men with dark skins, they're on the French side, but we have the Scots in kilts although they've got the Irish Catholics, we have the Protestant Irish and the Welsh . . . but the Portuguese fight on both sides.

CHUNTER: Just a minute, just a minute. If it came a fog, or a dust storm they wouldn't know who was fighting who.

GERVASE: You're right. And we could slip out in the middle and run for it.

CHUNTER: Don't look now, but the hills. Clouds.

GERVASE: I think you're right. It's the wind. We're in for a dust storm, they do blow in these parts.

CHUNTER: Gervase. If it comes a dust storm . . .

GERVASE: Yes.

CHUNTER: Remember one thing.

GERVASE: What's that?

CHUNTER: Whether they're Germans, or Russians, men in kilts or in bright trews, whether Catholic, Methodist, or Protestant, whether black or white, just remember, this fat thing is on your side.

GERVASE: It's coming, we'll stick together.

IT'S SUDDENLY DARK. GREAT WIND. THE DUST STORM. ENTER MANUEL, SPANISH SOLDIER, WHIPPING AROUND, SINGING AND SHOUTING. HE KEEPS CHANGING HATS AND VOICES.

VOICE: I belong to Glasgow, dear old Glasgow town . . .

GERVASE: A Scot.

WIND GUST. MANUEL DODGES AWAY.

VOICE: Paris. Paris. Vive la French. Alouetta . . .

CHUNTER: No. I think you're wrong, he's French.

WIND GUST. THEY PEER FOR MANUEL.

VOICE: Sole mia, haha, Parle Italiano, si si . . .

GERVASE: With Italian descent.

WIND GUST. MANUEL SCUDS ABOUT.

VOICE: Rossia, Roossia, hail the Csar. Moscow for ever.

CHUNTER: He's Russian.

THEY MEET.

GERVASE: Halt. Stand and turn round quietly.

CHUNTER: You better do it, he's as fierce as a bull.

THE SPANIARD DOES SO TREMBLINGLY.

MANUEL: Hah, English?

GERVASE: Yes.

CHUNTER: Dorset.

MANUEL: Doorstep. I know Doorstep. A great town. London eh? You know London?

GERVASE: We're countrymen, but we know London.

MANUEL: A great town London. I love London. St Pauls eh, St Pauls?

GERVASE: St Pauls. Yes.

MANUEL: Hah, Parliament eh? Parliament?

GERVASE: You're English too?

MANUEL: Am I English? Ha ha. Look, am I English. I have the hat to prove it.

English hat.

CHUNTER: That's a German hat.

MANUEL: Oh, wrong hat. I capture German hat because I'm gallant Britisher. Here, English hat.

GERVASE: He's English.

CHUNTER: He's a very sunburnt English.

GERVASE: Look here old chap. Are you quite certain you're English?

MANUEL: Oh, quite certain. The Queen eh? (SINGS.) God save our Gracious Queen.

GERVASE: It isn't Queen. It's King.

MANUEL: Hoh. Oh. I see. The Queen is dead is she? I been out here fighting such a long time. The Queen is dead? Muerte?

GERVASE: The last Queen we had has been dead near a hundred years.

MANUEL (CRIES): Hah, she was a lovely Queen. Well, I'm going back to my British ranks. The thin red line. I put my hat on and go back to fight for that King.

GERVASE: Stop friend. You aren't English.

MANUEL: Not English? You must be mad. Don't I know St Pauls? Parliament? God save the Queen or King. Not English? I know your Doorstep.

CHUNTER: Dorset.

MANUEL: That's it, that's it. Doorstep.

CHUNTER: We're friends pal. But you're not English. What are you?

MANUEL: You friends?

GERVASE: The best of friends. What are you?

MANUEL: Shall I tell you?

GERVASE: Yes.

MANUEL: You won't do me violence? Shot me? Stab me?

CHUNTER: Nothin' mate. We're in this against my will. What are you?

MANUEL: By birth sir, I am Spanish; but by nature and disposition I am peace loving to all my fellow men.

GERVASE: Well said. And so are we friend. What is your name?

MANUEL: My name is Manuel.

GERVASE: I am Gervase Becket the man who changed places, this is Chunter.

MANUEL: I love you both. Chunter, I could kiss you Chunter.

CHUNTER: Steady on, this is how I got here. Kissing sergeants.

GERVASE: Tell us your story Manuel. How you came to be here.

THEY CROUCH TOGETHER IN A CORNER.

MANUEL: I will, listen to this. This is my story. Look at these legs, have you ever seen such beautiful legs? But have you eh? Such lovely legs as these? Have you ever seen such.

GERVASE: No. Come to think. I haven't.

CHUNTER: Lemme see, lemme see. No, I haven't seen such spindles.

GERVASE: What do your legs do to be so important?

MANUEL: Sir. I am Manuel Pabloese, the great dancer.

BOTH: Dancer.

MANUEL: Dancer.

CHUNTER: Dancers must be well paid.

MANUEL: In Spain, Chunter, dancers are Gods, and none better than Manuel Pabloese, the great, thus . . . THUS, and thus . . . (HE STANDS UP AND DANCES.)

SHOOTING BREAKS OUT.

CHUNTER: Can you do the Hereford Barn Dance?

GERVASE: Get down Chunter.

CHUNTER: I'm showing him the steps.

SHOTS.

GERVASE: Get down or you'll be shot.

MORE SHOTS. THEY DIVE FOR COVER.

CHUNTER: Dance is over.

GERVASE: Go on Manuel.

MANUEL: So, I go round dancing; then one day in Seville, I am invited into a splendid house, to dance and instruct the girl of the house.

CHUNTER: Haaah, a girl.

MANUEL: Sylvette. My beautiful Sylvette. We dance; her feet are so light, we are dancing on the star, we are dancing in the clouds . . . then her father's voice brings me back to earth . . . 'You want to marry my Sylvette? All right,' he says, 'what do you bring my daughter?' And I say, 'The money I have is the money my legs earn for me, all the honour, title and position I have in life are won by my legs and feet.' And he says, 'Not enough for my Sylvette.'

GERVASE: How did you get here then?

MANUEL: He sent me. He says, 'You need a rank, honour, position to bring to my daughter. I'll get you in the army. Then you return, marry Sylvette.'

GERVASE: So you joined?

MANUEL: But it was all a trick. I joined. I said, 'You make me an officer?' They said, 'We make you nothing. We send you to battle to dance in front of the English army's musket balls,' and so, they put me in the thick of the battle . . .

GERVASE: But your Sylvette's father? His promise?

MANUEL: It was a trick. To get rid of me. And I have since heard he has arranged for my Sylvette to marry a dirty old Count.

CHUNTER: A Count? Phew. That's high.

MANUEL: Her father brought her a rumour that I had been killed. If I can only keep alive. Keep friendly with everyone, change my hats, be on all sides, get back to Madrid, just tell her that I am alive, then perhaps we can run away with each other.

GERVASE: If there's anything we can do.

CHUNTER: Anything at all.

MANUEL: Just pray that my beautiful legs do not get damaged, my friends.

GERVASE: We'll pray for that. Follow me.

MANUEL: Which way?

GERVASE: Under cloak of darkness.

MANUEL: But where?

GERVASE: Where is Sylvette?

MANUEL: Madrid.

GERVASE: Then that is where we're going.

THEY LISTEN. IT'S QUIET.

Ho, on we go, the war is over.

THEY SET OFF. ENTER SOLDIER, DONE UP AS A FRENCHMAN.

SOLDIER: Vive la France. Vive le roi. Paris, le Seine, vive la Compagnie . . .

SINGS A BAR. VIVE LA COMPAGNIE.

GERVASE: Listen. A Frenchman.

THEY STOP.

CHUNTER: One of them.

MANUEL: Leave it to me. Back me up with a bit of French. I'll put on a French hat. Back me up, chorus. Please.

CHUNTER AND GERVASE: Bonjour. Le Jour. Monsieur. Paris. Oui. Oui. (ETC.

MANUEL: Is that all you know?

CHUNTER AND GERVASE: Oui. Oui. Oui.

MANUEL GETS UP.

MANUEL (PUTTING ON A FRENCH HAT): Vive la Compagnie, vive la France, vive la Compagnie . . . (SINGS AND DANCES.)

THE SOLDIER SHOOTS HIM IN THE LEGS. MANUEL GOES DOWN.

Hah, my legs, friends. My legs.

SOLDIER: No. I'll finish him off.

GERVASE: No, for God's sake. Leave him, he's a friend of ours.

SOLDIER: Nah, he's a Spaniard, an onion.

GERVASE: But if you're French, as your hat says you are, you're on his side.

SOLDIER: Nah, mate. I'm English. I'm from Fulham, London. I saw him with you and he'd got you over the border; you're in enemy lines. So I thought, 'He's captured them prisoners.' Then I had a brainwave, I'm good with the old Thinkbox, I thought, 'I'll put a French hat on and go and shoot the Spanish Onion,' so I did. Now I'll finish him off. Put him out of his misery.

GERVASE: DONT. Don't, we'll look after him.

SOLDIER: Well, here's a queer do.

GERVASE: We'll take him home.

SOLDIER: To Spain? But do you know what they do with you if you're caught.

GERVASE: No, what?

SOLDIER: They put you to the Inquisition.

GERVASE: Inquisition. I don't care about the Inquisition.

HUNTER: Hold it, hold it, whoaa, not so fast, what's the Inquisition, soldier. What does it do?

SOLDIER: Why, it's what they have. It's a torture chamber for all of them as aren't Catholics.

HUNTER: Catholics?

SOLDIER: Yeah, they've got this rack . . .

HUNTER: What's a rack?

SOLDIER: They tie you up, on this rack, and they stretch you until your body snaps . . .

MANUEL: Listen. We have no Inquisition. That was 16th century.

SOLDIER: That's an onion tale. Load of cobblers. Then there's the thumb-screw.

HUNTER: What's this thumbscrew?

SOLDIER: Why, they put your thumb in this little box thing, with a crew on, then they tighten the screw, and tighten until your thumb is all squashed . . . then there's the iron maiden.

HUNTER: What's this iron maiden?

SOLDIER: Well, it's a sort of hollow statue, with spikes in, and they open it, put you in, then close it . . . then there's . . .

HUNTER: No more. No more. All this if you aren't Catholic?

SOLDIER: Yes. And more.

HUNTER: Where do we turn Catholics?

SOLDIER: You suit yourself mates. But I'm off.

SHOOTING.

CHUNTER: It's all right mate, we're coming.

MANUEL: Gervase. Gervase. Don't leave me.

SOLDIER: Shall I put him out of his misery? It'd be a kindness.

CHUNTER: You seem a kind type.

GERVASE: Leave him Tommy.

SOLDIER: I'm off then.

CHUNTER: We're coming Tommy. We English must stick together.

MANUEL: Gervase. Take my place and look for Sylvette.

AUTOHARP CHORDS.

VOICE: Sir Gervase Becket. Step forward.

CHUNTER: God help us, take his place, them fatal words . . . with thumb-screws and racks and iron maidens. You worry about your legs, what about my thumbs?

SHOOTING AND CANNON.

SOLDIER: Look lads, it's hotting up. If we make a dash now, in three minutes we'll be safe beyond the lines drinking tea . . . how about it?

CHUNTER: I take two sugars.

GERVASE: Soldier. Thanks for coming to our rescue. But you must go back alone.

SOLDIER: How about you Fatty?

CHUNTER: Oh my God, have I got to keep a date with an iron maiden?

SOLDIER: See that belly button? That's where the first spike goes.

CHUNTER: Aw, Gawd help us.

SOLDIER: Good luck then lads. I wouldn't do this. Not for an onion.

HE GOES.

MANUEL: Gervase. Gervase. It's my legs, my beautiful legs.

CHUNTER: His legs, his legs. How about my thumbs? Belly buttons, bones?

MANUEL: Gervase. Have a look. Will I ever dance again? Will I ever see my Sylvette again?

GERVASE INSPECTS HIS LEGS.

GERVASE: We will take you back, to see your Sylvette. We will take you.

BIG EXPLOSION.

MANUEL: Haaah.

GERVASE: He's fainted.

CHUNTER: I'm about to follow him.

GERVASE: When it's dark, we'll go.

cene 15 JOURNEY ACROSS SPAIN

HUNTER (NARRATING): When it was dark, we went.

ERVASE: Take a grip on his arm.

HUNTER: I've had a grip on his arm.

ERVASE: Lift him on to your back.

HUNTER: You said we'd travel light.

ERVASE: Up.

THEY SUPPORT HIM BETWEEN THEM.

MANUEL: Aaah, my leg.

THEY TROT. CASTANETS MAKE A JOURNEY SOUND.

VOICE: Who goes there?

THEY STOP.

HUNTER: What's Spanish for cow? Moo.

VOICE: Haah, it's just a cow.

ERVASE: It's no good, we'll have to make him a stretcher.

HUNTER: What with?

ERVASE: Two guns and your coat.

HUNTER: I'm cold without a coat.

ERVASE: We'll run.

THEY SET OFF. CASTANETS.

Right, how's that? Better? Manuel, where are we?

MANUEL: We're in Mandala country.

HUNTER: What's Mandala country?

MANUEL: Brigands, villains, cutthroats.

HUNTER: At the double, out of the Mandala land.

HUNTER (AS NARRATOR): We went through mountain country, giving the slip to brigands, priests and Mandalas.

VOICE: Halt, who goes there?

THEY STOP.

MANUEL: Mandalas. Quick, hide.

ERVASE: Into this gorse bush.

THEY DIVE DOWN. CRUNCH SOUND,

HUNTER: Ouch, howl . . .

ERVASE: We're safe, they won't come in here.

HUNTER: I'm prickled.

VOICES MUMBLE IN SPANISH. SILENCE. THEY SET OFF.

CHUNTER: Up precipices, across grass lands, along dry river beds we went, heading for Madrid; out of the country of the Mandalas to the cutthroat gypsy territories . . .

THERE IS THE STRUMMING OF THE GUITAR. THEY STOP.

Listen, music. That sounds friendly. A dance.

MANUEL: No, that's the music of the Sevilliacoes, wild, dangerous gypsy bands that roam round here.

VOICE: Alt! Ooo go there?

MANUEL: That's a Sevilliaco.

GERVASE: Quick, hide, into this river.

THEY DIVE. SPLASH.

CHUNTER: Ugh. I thought the water was warm in Spain.

SPANISH VOICES. SILENCE. THEY TROT AGAIN.

CHUNTER (AS NARRATOR): We dragged ourselves out of the water ten miles downstream, ran through the midnight air; till it seemed we must be getting near to somewhere . . .

VOICE: Who goes there?

THEY STOP.

CHUNTER: Not again, don't the villains ever sleep in Spain? What's this one?

MANUEL: Quick, hide, Cardinal's Guard . . . over this cliff.

THEY DIVE. CONFUSION. CLOAKED SPANIARDS RUSH ON AND FIRE AT EACH OTHER. EXIT CURSING. CHUNTER APPEARS.

CHUNTER (AS NARRATOR): We fell to the bottom of the cliff, where there was a farm. We couldn't deny our weary bones a rest. We found the barn and crawled into the hay, but one of us had to be sent to find food and water. Guess who.

Scene 16 THE FARM

DARK. GERVASE AND MANUEL APPEAR IN STRAW. A LANTERN.

MANUEL: I can't go on Gervase. I can't go on. My spirit flickers out like a candle in the wind.

GERVASE: Be brave Manuel. Here, rest. If you knew the fear that Chunter goes through over the Spanish Inquisition.

MANUEL: But there is no Spanish Inquisition.

GERVASE: I would like to take your word for it, friend. He wakes up in the night, calling out, 'Oh, my thumb,' or 'The Iron Maiden.' I have heard him, night after night, calling out, 'Oh, I'm stretched, oh, the Iron Maiden has me in her grip.'

MANUEL: I am sorry Gervase. Deeply contrite. I am sorry. I was sorrowful, that's all. About my legs, I was sorrowful.

ERVASE: All right, sleep. Goodnight my friend.

ANUEL: Goodnight my dear Gervase.

THE LIGHTS GO OUT. SILENCE. DIM LIGHT. ENTER CHUNTER IN THE DARK WITH FARM GIRL.

ERVASE: Chunter.

HUNTER: Gervase. Lights out?

ERVASE: Where have you been?

HUNTER: To a little farm. I have some food for you. We'll have a breakfast in the morning.

ERVASE: Do you want some light, while you undress?

HUNTER: No, I don't need the help of a light to undress.

LAUGHS. FROM THE GIRL.

ERVASE: I thought I heard laughs.

HUNTER: No. It was a sigh. I was sighing for old England.

ERVASE: Never mind brave Chunter, we'll be back there someday. And you can have your wenches and maids again.

GIRL PINCHES CHUNTER. CHUNTER 'OOCHES'.

What was that 'ooch' Chunter?

HUNTER: I pinched my foot taking my boots off.

ERVASE: I see. Goodnight then.

HUNTER: Goodnight.

ERVASE: What are you rolling and fidgeting about for in that straw?

HUNTER: I'm just getting comfy.

ERVASE: What did they give you at the farmhouse?

HUNTER: Oh, cider and bread, some cheese. For our breakfast.

ERVASE: You were always good with farmers. Did he have a wife?

HUNTER: An older lady.

ERVASE: You like them young. Did he have a daughter?

HUNTER: Well, he did have something that might pass for a daughter, but such an ugly, dowdy thing she was to tell you the truth. Ouch.

ERVASE: What was that 'ouch' for?

HE PUTS THE LIGHT ON, SEES CHUNTER WITH HIS GIRL.

HUNTER: Hah, your touch is like exquisite pain.

ERVASE: Chunter, I thought you were having a nightmare.

HUNTER: My sleeping times are no concern of yours.

ERVASE: Chunter, who is this woman?

CHUNTER: I went to the farm, I was given bread, meat and cheese, I was given milk to drink and a little cider; these I will share with you in the morning; b any other little titbits I keep to myself. Now, goodnight.

BLOWS OUT THE CANDLE.

Scene 17 OUTSIDE SYLVETTE'S HOUSE

A COCK CROWS.

CHUNTER (AS NARRATOR): Well, the next day, up at cock crow and off. Another wench left behind us. We reached Madrid eventually, and there, as planned, left Manuel with friends, and went to the house of Sylvette – such a house, a mansion, and packed with servants. The place was humming with life when we got there.

A CREEPER HANGING DOWN, DECORATED WITH FLOWERS. GERVASE JOINS HIM. ENTER SERVANT WOMAN, LADEN WITH STUFF.

GERVASE: Say friend . . . Senora.

SERVANT WOMAN: Out of the way, out of it, can you not see I'm busy? Who are you? What are you idling at?

CHUNTER: Excitable, excitable. Just like Manuel.

SERVANT WOMAN: Manuel? I know no Manuel.

GERVASE: What goes on friend?

SERVANT WOMAN: Wedding. Wedding. Hah, the bride from the House, Miss Sylvette . . .

GERVASE: Who to?

SERVANT WOMAN: To a Count eh, that's life friend. We poor, marry the poor; but the rich, they marry counts. It's a great day for the happy groom, and Sylvette . . . (SHRUGS.) Beauty must marry money.

GERVASE: But Chunter, it doesn't seem right. To forget Manuel already, for a Count. It sounds wrong. She must be up there somewhere, behind one of those windows.

CHUNTER: I can see at least five thousand windows up there. What do we do? Throw a stone at every one till a beautiful girl appears. More likely the Inquisition.

ENTER SECOND SERVANT, MAN, LADEN.

SECOND SERVANT: Out of the way, out of it, can you not see I'm busy? Hi hi . . .

GERVASE: Friend. Isn't that Miss Sylvette's window open up there. Won't she catch a chill?

SERVANT: Chill?

GERVASE: Or sunstroke. Look, her window's open.

SERVANT: Where? I don't see her window open.

GERVASE: That one, there, that's her window.

SERVANT: Pooh, that's her window there. The one with the creeper up to it, let me see, one floor, two floors, five floors up.

CHUNTER: That's a big climb.

GERVASE: I see the one. Sorry I was wrong friend.

SECOND SERVANT GOES.

Up we go Chunter.

CHUNTER: Up you go Gervase. I'm not built for climbing.

GERVASE: All right. But if the Inquisition are prowling about, don't tell them about me. Even under torture.

CHUNTER: I'm climbing.

THEY CLIMB UP THE CREEPER.

Scene 18 UP THE CREEPER

CHUNTER: Hi, Gervase. Bit high aren't we?

GERVASE: I think it was the next window.

CHUNTER: Think she lives on the roof, do you? Or are we bird nesting?

GERVASE: Do you think we have passed it?

CHUNTER: I'm sure we have. Shhh. Listen, sounds below. Room below. Gervase. Sighing . . .

GERVASE: Can you *see* into it?

CHUNTER: Haaaah, yes, glimpse of white dress, no . . .

GERVASE: Get in then, let's get in. Down we go.

CHUNTER: It might be a trap, Gervase. It might be Inquisition men in white. I think they wear white for their butchery.

GERVASE: No. I heard a sigh that time. Get on in.

CHUNTER: Gervase . . . change places with me.

GERVASE: Oh, all right, hang on with your teeth.

CHUNTER: I am, and toenails and all.

GERVASE CLIMBS DOWN.

Scene 19 SYLVETTE

GERVASE: Psst. Miss.

SYLVETTE: Oh, who are you? Who sent you? My father. I know. My father sent you to spy on me.

GERVASE: No, no, Senorita. He didn't send us.

SYLVETTE: There's another one. Who's he?

GERVASE: He's a friend. He's having difficulty climbing the iron work.

CHUNTER CLIMBS DOWN.

SYLVETTE: Get back down. Immediately.

CHUNTER: I like that. I really do. I love that. We spend half an hour, and much skin off our knuckles getting up. And all she can say is . . .

SYLVETTE: Get back down immediately.

CHUNTER: That's all she's got to say. Will nobody in this life show a bit of consideration? I like that. We go round doing good turns, we change places with beggars, they have the coats from our backs, the food from our mouths, they shoot at us, punch us, starve us, we climb up creepers for them . . .

SYLVETTE: He's violent.

GERVASE: Let him let off steam Senorita. He's been through a strain.

CHUNTER: Then we get to Spain, bang bang, try to shoot fatty, then along comes Manuel . . .

SYLVETTE: Manuel?

CHUNTER: I said Manuel.

SYLVETTE: You know Manuel?

CHUNTER: Know Manuel? Did we make a stretcher for him out of our own jackets? Didn't we lug him over the countryside? But Manuel he says 'go and find my Sylvette' so, to Sylvette's house we go. Why do they have such high windows to these houses? Up, up, up, skin off my knuckles, terrific height, look down, all dizzy. Scramble in to safety, and SHE SAYS, 'Get back down immediately.'

SYLVETTE: Manuel. You've come from Manuel then?

GERVASE: Yes. We've come from Manuel.

SYLVETTE: How is he? Tell me how he is.

GERVASE: First, tell us how you feel about him?

SYLVETTE: Manuel? Oh, he is so beautiful, he has a body like a God, and black hair like a raven, and he is happy, and . . . full of life, and such legs, and dancing . . . haaah.

GERVASE: But, just say, if his legs and dancing, if they were gone. What then?

SYLVETTE: His legs? His dancing? Gone?

GERVASE: If his legs were stiff, or lost, and he couldn't dance?

SYLVETTE: I would still love that Manuel.

GERVASE: Haaah, then we can take you to him. But, prepare for the shock, thanks to your father, he has been injured in the legs and won't be dancing again.

SYLVETTE: I wouldn't mind that, for Manuel.

GERVASE: Then slip on a cloak, and we'll take you to him.

SYLVETTE: Hoh. And who will marry the Count?

AUTOHARP CHORDS. NO VOICE THIS TIME.

GERVASE: Never fear, we will find a bride to replace you.

SYLVETTE: How?

GERVASE: An idea always comes before morning. Now, you must go to Manuel. Tell him you were sent by Gervase Becket, the man who changed places. Englishman.

SYLVETTE: Englishman?

CHUNTER: Doorstep.

SYLVETTE: How can I thank you? Both?

CHUNTER: If I wasn't like your Count, old, wrinkled, toothless, paunchy, you could thank me easily.

SHE KISSES HIM.

SYLVETTE: You are lovable. My Count isn't.

CHUNTER: Once more. That last time caught me unawares.

SHE KISSES HIM.

GERVASE: Go quickly, collect your maid and then reach Manuel.

SHE GOES.

CHUNTER: Well, master, in the morning, they'll be tapping on that door, asking for a blushing bride; and what do they get? Us?

GERVASE: Something will come out.

CHUNTER: Something will come out all right, fingernails, eyes, teeth; something will come off, head.

GERVASE: It is all for the cause Chunter. Now I must sleep.

HE SLEEPS.

Haaah, the rack. Oh the torture. Don't stretch, don't stretch. I'm snapping. Oh the pain. Where is the Iron Maiden?

CHUNTER: He dreams, not the dreams I had with my farm wench. Just the dreams of his iron maiden. Poor Gervase.

Scene 20 THE STREET

MUSIC. CROWD SOUNDS.

MANUEL (ALONE): Music. Festivities. Must there be music to mock me all the days of my life? What can I do with music? Better they'd made me deaf as well, block out the music. That's a dance I know well they're playing in the streets. It's a marriage dance. That coach. That coach is Sylvette's. She is getting married then? Haaah, Sylvette; they are dancing at your wedding . . . I thought once, that we would dance at our wedding . . . there she goes, in her coach . . . I can't look . . .

COACH SOUND. ENTER SYLVETTE, IN CLOAK.

SYLVETTE: Manuel.

MANUEL: Sylvette. But you're in the coach. I've seen you. There. Can you be in two places at once?

SYLVETTE: I do not know who that is, but I am here.

MANUEL: I thought they were dancing at your wedding.

SYLVETTE: They think they are. But a brave Englishman, Sire Gervase Becket, said he would find another bride for them. I am for you Manuel. And I will only dance again when I marry you.

MANUEL: Is that a promise?

SYLVETTE: It is a promise.

MANUEL: One day, I will dance again. Oh Sylvette. (EMBRACE.) Listen, the Cathedral bells, they're entering the Church. Who were you supposed to be marrying?

SYLVETTE: Count Picasto.

MANUEL: That wrinkled, toothless, pot-bellied repulsive reptile. Then who can Gervase persuade to marry him?

SYLVETTE: I do not know. But whoever she is, I pity her, and thank her with all my heart.

Scene 21 THE WEDDING

CATHEDRAL. ALTAR. ENTER PRIEST. ENTER GERVASE DRESSED AS SYLVETTE, SYLVETTE'S FATHER, OLD COUNTY, GUARD, CHUNTER IN BACKGROUND.

PRIEST: I now call thee, in the presence of the people of Madrid and in the eyes of God, Man and Wife. You may kiss the bride.

COUNT: May I?

PRIEST: You may.

COUNT: Lift up your veil, my love, that I may see your sweet red lips, your black soft eyes, your skin like the blush of a plum . . . lift.

FATHER: You must obey your husband my dear.

GERVASE DOES SO. PANDEMONIUM.

COUNT: Arrgh!

PRIEST: Diable!

FATHER: Supplice!

GUARD: Carumba!

CHUNTER: Urgh!

GERVASE: I am Gervase Becket, Englishman. This buffoon was to have married the most beautiful girl in Spain, shame on you all; look at him, he

is ticking with dropsy, his eyes are wet and watery, his lips . . . ughhh.

THER: Where is my daughter?

RVASE: Fled, to the man she loves. She may be poor, but she will be happy, and married to a man of her own YOUTH. I could not let her marry this old, hot Harry.

THER: To the Inquisition with him.

UNT: No. No. Let me have him. I married him. I have merchant ships, rowed by galley slaves. Let me put him there for a number of years while I decide how he is to die.

RVASE: You see, THIS IS THE DEVIL you would have married to your daughter, sir.

UNT: Take him. I will have him lashed every mile to Morocco.

RVASE: Nautical mile? Or English mile?

THEY GO. IN UPROAR. CLUBBING GERVASE ABOUT.

UNTER (TO AUDIENCE): Do you see how I slipped unnoticed in the melé? Disguised as I am, artfully, as the lady's maid, I'll now dodge off to Manuel, and tell him the news.

ne 22 THE GALLEY

BOARD THE GALLEY. SLAVES ARE CHAINED FROM LEFT TO
GHT, THUS: NEGRO (LUMBA) . . . BLANK SEAT . . . OFFICER (OF THE
GILISTIC ENCOUNTER). OARS ARE UP IN AIR. GERVASE IS BRUTALLY
OUGHT IN BY AN ARAB CAPTAIN.

PTAIN: Your hand.

HOLDS OUT MANACLES.

RVASE: And yours sir. Delighted.

GERVASE HOLDS OUT HAND FOR HANDSHAKE.

PTAIN: Get these on. Down to your place.

HE MANACLES GERVASE. GERVASE IS COCKY.

RVASE: Thank you. Anyone for a row? Threepence an hour. We could use
you in our park, on the paddleboats. Come in number seven. Time's up!

CAPTAIN HITS HIM WITH THE BACK END OF A WHIP.

Hit a man when he's manacled would you.

PTAIN: One more empty place to be filled, then we go.

HE GOES.

RVASE: Morning all, piped aboard. Anymore for a trip round the bay?
When we sailing lads? Keeps you in trim a bit of pulling at the oar. I used to
pull for my old college. Well, chaps do we introduce ourselves?

MBA: The newcomers are always cheerful. Their spirits soon drop.

GERVASE: Oh, not at all, not at all. I'll keep my pecker up.

OFFICER: I know that voice.

GERVASE: Who said that behind?

LUMBA: You're not allowed to turn brother. You just look at the back of the man in front of you until one day . . .

GERVASE: One day, yes?

LUMBA: He drops down and dies over his oar.

GERVASE: Oh, come on, it can't be as bad as that can it? A bit of a pull at the old oar?

LUMBA: It's as bad as that sir. Lift it.

GERVASE: Surely. I can handle an oar. (TRIES TO LIFT IT.) Can't budge it, they must have it chained down somewhere.

LUMBA: It ain't chained friend. Lift it.

GERVASE: Help. I can't move it.

LUMBA: It's coming. It's coming.

GERVASE: This isn't an oar, it's a treetrunk.

OFFICER: I know that voice. I could swear I know that voice.

LUMBA: When the wind is high against you, and the storm lashing, the Driver's whip is lashing, you'll use that oar like a matchstick.

GERVASE: You keep cheerful friend, what's your name?

LUMBA: Lumba.

GERVASE: What's your other name Lumba? Other name. You must have another name?

LUMBA: I have indeed sir. Blind Lumba.

GERVASE: Blind Lumba? I didn't know. I'm sorry.

LUMBA: So am I sir, but there's nothing I can do about it. At least it saves me seeing your back when the muscles are standing out with the strain, and when the red lines appear where the whips have been, and the shoulders hunch, and the spirit breaks. And the strength is gone.

GERVASE: And what happens when the strength is gone?

LUMBA: Sir, they put you over the side.

GERVASE: Surely they can't be that cruel?

OFFICER: I know that damned voice.

GERVASE: They can't be that cruel Lumba?

LUMBA: Yes indeed they can be sir. I had eyes when I first came on this place.

GERVASE: You had eyes.

LUMBA: But those eyes once saw the mountains of home and they conveyed

a message to this brain and this brain said, 'Go Lumba,' and I got free, and
went, but I couldn't travel far in my irons, and they caught me up in the
jungle, and they said, 'Where are you going?' And I said, 'My eyes saw home,'
and they said, 'Not no more, they won't see home no more,' and they took
them away.

RVASE: You're very brave, to have such spirit. You are a philosopher
friend.

FICER: I know your voice.

RVASE: I don't know yours friend. And I can't see your face.

FICER: I have it, are you the man who goes round boasting that he changes
places?

RVASE: I don't remember boasting friend. But I change places with those
people who regret their own place.

FICER: Haaah, I know you now. How I hate you.

RVASE: Hate me? Friend, that's a thing I've never had in my life. Hate.

FICER: I hate you.

MBA: Why do you hate him?

FICER: Haaah, not long ago, less than a year if memory serves me right, I
was a happy man, dressed in blue and gold uniform . . . and you have
brought me to this.

RVASE: I know, the Cavalry Officer.

FICER: Yes, the Cavalry Officer.

RVASE: If only people would be content with the position in life that God
has given them, then they could only blame either themselves, for the mess
they make, or accept their lot, as divine Providence.

MBA: Now there are two philosophers on this oar bench.

FICER: Look, here comes a rich man.

RVASE: Why is he coming here?

FICER: Why, to buy a slave.

TAIN (SHOUTS): Ayee Aa.

MBA: That means 'silence'.

ENTER CHUNTER, DRESSED AS A RICH MERCHANT.

UNTER: Hi, pipe me aboard then.

TAIN: What do you want here?

UNTER: I've come to buy a slave.

TAIN: It costs gold to buy a slave from this bench.

UNTER: I haven't come light.

TAIN: What sort of slave do you want? Size? Shape?

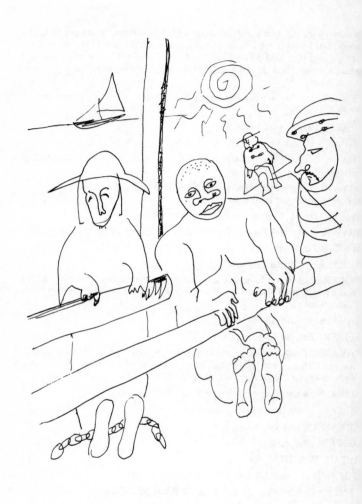

HUNTER: Oh, I have in mind something long and thin, suitable for reaching up to tall clothes lines; nothing squat or fat, one that would change places at the drop of a pot of gold . . .

GERVASE: Chunter . . .

HUNTER: I could pass my mother in this disguise, master. They look a sturdy lot here, captain.

CAPTAIN: They have to be sturdy. Or, pchaa, over the side.

HUNTER: What happened to the man in this place?

CAPTAIN: He wasn't sturdy.

HUNTER: So, pchaaa . . .

BOTH: Over the side.

HUNTER: So, you need a slave too, eh? I need a slave, you need a slave.

CAPTAIN: That is right, your Highness.

HUNTER: And when you fill this place?

CAPTAIN: Why, then I call out, 'Hoist the anchor and away!'

HUNTER: And that sends you scuttling, eh? When do you hope to do that? When the tide's right?

CAPTAIN: The tide is right. When I find a slave . . .

HUNTER: Hoist anchor and . . .

BOTH: Away . . .

HUNTER: Actually, it isn't a bad little spot this, for a man who doesn't have much ambition.

CAPTAIN: The man at that seat was quite contented with his square yard of dry board . . . he would have preferred it . . . to the ocean, with all its vastness.

HUNTER: Yes, may I? Curiosity. Tell the folks back home I've sat on a galley bench.

CAPTAIN: Please do, your Highness.

CHUNTER SITS IN EMPTY PLACE. FINGERS OAR.

HUNTER: The sort of chap you would need, to lift this, he'd have to be quite strong.

CAPTAIN: I can train him, your Highness.

HUNTER: And these manacles. Not very long, are they?

CAPTAIN: It keeps them near their work.

HUNTER: Suppose they can eat, drink, pick their nose, nothing much else needed in life, is there?

CAPTAIN: They lead a simple life, your Highness.

HUNTER: Right, I'll have my slave. I'll have him. When I get out of here. How much?

CHUNTER STANDS.

CAPTAIN: Why, the bag of gold.

CHUNTER: Too much by half. (HE SITS STUBBORNLY.)

CAPTAIN: But I take all, your Highness.

GERVASE TRIES TO WARN CHUNTER.

GERVASE: Chunter!

CAPTAIN FELLS CHUNTER WITH A BLOW FROM BEHIND.

CAPTAIN: Full crew! Hoist anchor and away!

WATER LAPPING SOUNDS.

GERVASE: What is your philosophy of that Lumba?

LUMBA: Never taste freedom until you've bit the earth.

GERVASE: And for Chunter? My friend.

THEY LOWER THE OARS.

LUMBA: Your friend?

GERVASE: He is my Chunter. A friend.

LUMBA: Haaah, well, fools rush in where wise men, nor rich men, would go.

GERVASE: We're away.

CAPTAIN: Row, you swine. Row. Row or I'll make your backs raw.

BEATING SOUND. THEY ROW IN TIME TO IT.

Scene 23 AT SEA

THEY ROW. IT GETS DARKER.

CHUNTER (AS NARRATOR): A few weeks later I looked like something that had taken a body building course. I had muscles where I didn't know muscles grew. Even my moustache had muscles. The life was very simple, you simply pulled at your oar. If it rained you opened your mouth and drank, they fed you on dry bread and rotten meat to keep your strength up. If the wind blew up and filled the sails, lucky us, we had a rest; if another ship chased us then we all rowed like merry Hell because if the ship went down in a fight, we went down with it. The Officer beside me was never happy; but Lumba, he was always cheerful, and would keep us going with his homespun philosophy.

THEY SIT LAUGHING. ALONG COMES THE CAPTAIN AND WHIPS THEM.

GERVASE: What was that for friend?

CAPTAIN: Nothing.

GERVASE: What happens when we do something?

CAPTAIN: I kill you twice as bad.

LUMBA: A man can only die once.

CAPTAIN: Time I've finished with you you'll want to be dead.

LUMBA: No sir, I like life. I like my brethren. Even the whipwielders.

CAPTAIN WHIPS HIM AGAIN AND GOES.

HUNTER: For once Lumba, I would have changed places with you.

LUMBA: There is a story. The whip that is meant for you lands on your own back and no other.

GERVASE: A good proverb.

CAPTAIN (SHOUTS): Ba-eee-aa.

SLAVES PUT OARS UP. BEATING STOPS.

LUMBA: Now friends, I have something to give you.

GERVASE: Give us? What can you give us? Fresh air? Advice? You have nothing else.

LUMBA: This.

HE HANDS THEM A SMALL FILE.

GERVASE: A file.

LUMBA: You remember. I escaped. But I had my chains around me, and they caught me, but I swore, if there was ever a next time, I would not have chains. I secured this file, but they put my eyes out, for escaping. I swore, that if I ever met men who deserved freedom, they would have it. Take it. No one deserves it more.

HUNTER: A file. Hide it.

LUMBA: When darkness comes, file your bonds loose. And when the day comes, when you can see land, jump over the side and swim for freedom.

GERVASE: But you, my friend.

LUMBA: No, I have long since decided. Freedom is not for me.

GERVASE: Then, as you have given it to us, may we be worthy of freedom Lumba.

LUMBA: Remember, keep it hidden. The penalty for escape is blindness. And I couldn't bear to make anyone else like myself.

GERVASE: We'll risk it, and always remember.

OFFICER: What's that? I heard. A file? Give it here. Give it me. You said you would change places. Give it to me. I demand it. I can use freedom more than any other man. Give it here. You got me into this, now get me out. Give it to me, or I'll shout for the Driver.

HUNTER: Filing is hard work anyway. And Gervase can only back paddle, who wants to back paddle all the way to Africa.

OFFICER: Give it here, quickly.

LUMBA: Friend. I do not think you are worthy of taking the freedom from these men. They have given you everything, and you blame them for your own misfortune.

OFFICER: Give it here, or I shout for the Driver.

GERVASE: Here it is. What must be . . . must be.

THEY PASS ON THE FILE. ENTER CAPTAIN. IT GETS DARKER.

CAPTAIN: One of you is in possession of a file.

CHUNTER: How did he know that?

LUMBA: On this bench you cannot even THINK a secret.

CAPTAIN: So one of you would escape, would you? One of you would see the land and depart? Well, ask that man what the reward is for escape. Ask that man. He once saw the land, now he sees nothing.

HE GOES.

OFFICER: Oh, my God, my eyes. Blindness. No. No. Never. I cannot. No. I cannot. I'd rather be a slave to this bench for the rest of my days than lose my eyes like Lumba. Sir, take it, you must take it.

GERVASE: This is a changeable man.

OFFICER: Take it. I cannot face what they'll do to my eyes. Please. I was here when they blinded Lumba, oh God, please. Please.

CHUNTER: This man is a changeable coward who wants every way out.

GERVASE: Here, put yourself out of your misery. I cannot let you suffer like this. But know that, that the man who could never face his own fate in life, didn't deserve living.

OFFICER: Oh, God, rid of it. I'll remember. I'll remember. I'm just a worm who clings on to life.

ENTER CAPTAIN.

CAPTAIN: Well, let the search begin. But the irons are in the fire.

TERRIFIC WIND BLOWS.

CRIES: Typhoon. Typhoon.

GERVASE: Chunter, the file. The file.

CRASH. CONFUSION. OARS AND BITS OF SHIP DISPERSE.

Scene 24 ENGLISH SHIP

CHUNTER (AS NARRATOR, OVER THE STORM): At that moment one of the dreaded typhoons blew up. Gervase and I freed ourselves with the file. The last thing I remember was Gervase trying to free Lumba but Lumba shouting, 'No, save yourselves, save yourselves.' There was a terrific crash as the mast snapped and then I must have been struck a blow on the head, because the next thing I knew was that I was lying in the cabin of a ship. Gervase was standing, wrapped in silence and thought.

STORM HAS ENDED. CHUNTER IS LYING DOWN. GERVASE IS STRANGELY SILENT.

What is this then? Was it all a dream Gervase?

GERVASE: No dream.

CHUNTER: Gervase, Gervase. What happened?

SILENCE. ENTER FRIENDLY CAPTAIN, A QUAKER. CREAKING. DISTANT BELL-BUOY.

ENGLISH CAPTAIN: So, you're awake.

CHUNTER: Where's your whip? Bring out your whip.

ENGLISH CAPTAIN: There is no whip, friend. Can I bring you tea? Buttered scones? Or toast and jam?

CHUNTER: No. Not yet. Tell me friend, where are we? Where are we bound? What happened?

ENGLISH CAPTAIN: We are on the good ship, MARIAN, named after my dear beloved wife; we are in the English Channel, we are bound for the Port of London, hah, and as for what happened, I was sailing off the coast of Africa when I came upon a tremendous typhoon . . .

CHUNTER: Yes. Yes. We met it.

ENGLISH CAPTAIN: I weathered it, through the mercy of God, with all sails lashed down and our bow facing into the waves. When it passed by, for I can't say we passed through it, I came across the wreckage of a ship, but clinging to a mast I saw one figure, your friend; and beside him, another figure tied to the mast, yourself . . .

CHUNTER: I don't remember.

ENGLISH CAPTAIN: You were unconscious. And have been for many days.

CHUNTER: Many days?

ENGLISH CAPTAIN: Yes, indeed. Many days. Your friend, well, he has been conscious all of the time, indeed has never lost consciousness, even to sleep. So, I have been in charge of the living and the dead.

CHUNTER: But Gervase, he is usually so talkative.

ENGLISH CAPTAIN: Then he may have had a knock on the head, for he isn't talkative now.

GERVASE: Lumba, there is one thing left that I must do.

CHUNTER: This is no knock on the head.

GERVASE: There is one thing I left that I must do.

CHUNTER: What is it that you must do Gervase?

GERVASE: Lumba would know. Lumba would know, there is one thing left that I must do.

CHUNTER: We're on our way home master, England, in the company of this good captain here. Lumba would understand that we are right to go home, wouldn't he?

GERVASE: I know now what I must do Chunter. Lumba pointed me the way.

ENGLISH CAPTAIN: What did Lumba do?

GERVASE: He died for us. He gave up his life for ours.

Scene 25 THE GALLOWS

DRUM BEATS.

CHUNTER (AS NARRATOR): This is all Gervase could be made to say; then when we reached London, he was still in a trance. And with long strides off he went. I trotted on behind him, saying, 'Master, where are we going? What are we looking for?' and all he would say was, 'There is one more thing, for Lumba.' Then we reached Tyburn, where the gallows were set up, and looked up at a prisoner who was to be hung.

BUGLES PLAY FUNERAL FANFARE. ENTER CROWD. SOLDIERS, HANGMAN, CONDEMNED CRIMINAL.

CRIMINAL: I'm a poor thing. This is a miserable way to end a glorious life. Woe, lack a day. What a way to end up, dangling like a sack of potatoes, down there, feet first. It's horrible.

AUTOHARP CHORDS.

VOICE: Sir Gervase Becket. Step forward.

CHUNTER: Gervase. You aren't.

GERVASE: Didn't Lumba do it for us?

CHUNTER: Gervase. No, he's just a common criminal.

CRIMINAL: When I drop folks, give a cheer, just for me. I've never been applauded before. Give me a rousing drop, let my exit be joyous, because my birth was miserable.

GERVASE: Why, what did you do to deserve this friend? And why was your birth miserable?

CRIMINAL: My birth was miserable because I was born in the chains of poverty, and what I did to deserve this was to try to get out of poverty. Society had always its pockets full, mine were empty, so I had to pick from society.

GERVASE: In other words you were a pick-pocket?

CRIMINAL: I picked the purses out of society's back pocket. But now, I am at the moment, a trussed up bird. Ready for the final drop.

GERVASE: Would you like to change places with me friend?

CROWD LAUGHS DERISIVELY.

CRIMINAL: Well, there is a good crowd, and my fingers still itch. They have come to see my neck pinched, I would love to get among them and pinch them in their purses.

GERVASE: If I take your place, will you promise to try to earn a living? To go to my estate and work on the land?

CROWD: He's a crank, a madman, etc.

CRIMINAL: Have you an estate? You don't look like a man with an estate.

GERVASE: You don't look like a man ready to die. Is it a promise?

CRIMINAL: I'll promise anything.

CHUNTER: You bet he will.

GERVASE: And promise you'll be an honest man ever more and pick no more pockets?

CRIMINAL: I'm cured of picking pockets by your action. If there was a mousetrap, or a poison snake in each pocket, I couldn't be more cured.

GERVASE: May I take his place?

EXECUTIONER: We all have our places in the world, sir. Mine is to hang people, not to identify them. One neck is much like another.

GERVASE: I have seen a cobbler with more interest in his shoes than this tradesman has in his necks. All right, then, friend. Change places. Present yourself to Bailiff Grimthorpe at this address and farewell.

CRIMINAL: I'm off.

GERVASE: Aren't you staying to watch?

CRIMINAL: No sir, I'd feel it if I stayed. Thanks a lot sir. (TO CHUNTER.) Is he nuts?

CHUNTER: Either he is, or we all are.

CRIMINAL SKIPS OFF.

CRIMINAL: Here comes the Commander of the City Guard to officiate. I'm missing a date with him that I'd rather not have.

SOLEMN DRUMS. ENTER THE POLITE SERGEANT, NOW A MAN OF HIGH RANK. SOLDIERS COME TO ATTENTION.

SERGEANT: Well, prisoner, before the rope is pulled, would you like to say something?

GERVASE (TO CROWD): Yes, good people. Before my final moment comes . . . I should like to . . .

CHUNTER WEEPS.

I should like to say . . . I've learnt that . . . er . . . I should like to say . . .

CHUNTER: Say something important.

GERVASE: When you eat your sandwiches, keep the litter off the grass, and throw your crumbs to the birds, they've had a bad winter.

SERGEANT: I know that voice.

CHUNTER: Can't you say something noble and aspiring Gervase for your last moment?

GERVASE: I'm trying to. But can't. I can only think of mundane things to say. So, good people, if I'm wriggling about up there, as well I might, because I have a stringy neck, turn your children's eyes away, don't lose sleep over me, after the show tea is provided from yon tent.

SERGEANT: I know that voice. I know your voice. Yes. The highwayman.

GERVASE: The courteous Sergeant, my philosophical companion.

SERGEANT: Yes, I'm the Sergeant. But now a General, I've been promoted by the King to this high position . . . I am Commander General of this city.

GERVASE: You call this a high position? The six foot drop?

SERGEANT: This is the least savoury of my duties my friend . . . but when I can exercise my prerogative of mercy then it is a post fit for a philosopher. Now Gervase, you've been round the round world on your quest, I can either hang you, or free you. What is your decision? Have you fulfilled your mission?

GERVASE: Well Chunter, I'll leave the decision to you. Shall we call the mission closed? Or shall I be hung?

CHUNTER: Master, if it means going through all these adventures again I'd see you hanged; but if we can go home straight away, I'll have you cut down.

SERGEANT: Well Gervase?

GERVASE: Sergeant I set out on a journey full of a question, now I know the answer, and I know where I must go. Home, let me down.

THEY RELEASE GERVASE. FANFARE. CROWD DISPERSES. SCAFFOLD AWAY.

CHUNTER: One thing Gervase.

GERVASE: Yes?

CHUNTER: Is the adventure over? Now that you've been on the scaffold, is it all done? No more changing?

GERVASE: No more.

CHUNTER: What is ours, is ours? What we have we keep? What we own we don't give away?

GERVASE: Agreed.

CHUNTER: Then General, if you could let us have a couple of fast horses, there's a maid I would like to see.

SERGEANT: Anything is yours. Yes my friend, they shall be yours.

GERVASE: No Chunter; no horses. As we came out, so we go back. What is the last hundred miles after the distance we have covered?

CHUNTER: A quick walk Gervase. A quick walk.

JOURNEY MUSIC. THEY WALK.

Scene 26 THE RETURN

CHUNTER: And so, we bid farewell and set off back home, and believe me, I was more eager to go than when we set out. I was longing to see the well-kept farm, the spruce outbuildings, the neat orchards and tidy hedgerows; but when we approached, things seemed, to put it mildly, amiss . . .

MUSIC STOPS AFTER GETTING MISERABLE. ENTER PEASANT WITH RUSTY SCYTHE. RAGGED, STARVED LOOKING WIFE.

GERVASE: Hi, there, peasant. That's a rusty scythe you've got. You can't do an honest day's labour with that.

PEASANT: But I can keep you away with it. Go on, clear off.

GERVASE: Why, I heard this place once had a name for hospitality.

PEASANT: This place once had a name for a lot of things, work, honesty, hospitality, everything. But now . . .

GERVASE: What happened man?

PEASANT: We were a thriving place, and had a reputation for hospitality but our damned master went off and sent this highwayman to live with us; he worked for a time, but soon resorted to his old ways; held us all up, robbed us inside out and then off he went with a new mask and a brace of my old master's pistols . . .

CHUNTER (ASIDE): So much for the man who wanted to lead an honest life with the militia on his heels.

ENTER SECOND PEASANT WITH BROKEN RAKE. MORE RAGGED PEASANTS FOLLOW.

GERVASE: Peasant, is that food you have there, for a pair of travellers?

SECOND PEASANT: Food? On this farm? Once we had food, oh once we had food; orchards, honey bees, hens' eggs . . . but our master went off and along came this glutton in his place to live with us; it wasn't long before he started nibbling this, and nibbling that; then he attacked the orchard, and the wine barrels, and cheese stores till he ate us out of house and home . . . there's no food in this farm.

CHUNTER: Our glutton was going to give up food so that he could be spry and stand on his hands. Hi, peasant, did he ever learn to stand on his hands?

SECOND PEASANT: Stand on his hands? They had to wheel him away in a specially made carriage with heavy springs . . .

ENTER THIRD PEASANT.

GERVASE: Peasant. Have you a place where we can rest our limbs for an hour.

THIRD PEASANT: Rest your limbs? On what? On chairs? On beds? You try to find them traveller. Our master forgot his responsibilities and went off and sent a soldier and his wife, name of Tommy Triplefoot, came on us to start a home; but they brought all of their relations, and other soldiers, and deserters; oh, the place was like a barracks; and when they went, they took everything along with them like an army on the move. Horses, carts, everything went . . .

CHUNTER: This is a pretty pass. I put skirts on for that man, and faced the grapeshot.

GERVASE: But where is your master?

ENTER BROKEN-DOWN GRIMTHORPE.

GRIMTHORPE: Master? We have no master sir. Once we had the best master in the world; the barns were full, the beasts fat and contented; there was drinking and skittle matches, the buildings were well kept; but he went barmy and changed places with me . . . and look at the pretty state things have come to.

AMELIA COMES FORWARD.

AMELIA: And our master took our fat Chunter, who was the merriest and gayest of men, who kept us all happy . . . but now, oh we wish we could have him back . . .

GRIMTHORPE: We wish we could have Chunter back sir, and our master in his right mind again.

PEASANTS GENERALLY NOD AND AGREE.

GERVASE: Friends, perhaps we can bring them back.

GRIMTHORPE: But who are you.

GERVASE (WHIPPING OFF HIS HAT): Gervase Becket, the man who changed places, and came back wiser.

AMELIA: And this one?

CHUNTER: Chunter Hodges, the fat man who went with him, and came back thinner.

PEASANTS TAKE OFF CAPS. GRIMTHORPE KNEELS. THE OTHERS FOLLOW SUIT.

GERVASE: Up off your knees people. The thing I have learned is to envy no man; and bend the knee to no man. We must all work together, and rebuild our farm, reseed our land, replant our trees, restock our beasts . . . It is not for you to kneel, but for me to beg you to take me back.

AS A REPLY, PEASANTS RISE AND LINE UP IN TWO OPPOSITE AND FACING LINES WITH CHUNTER AND GERVASE IN BETWEEN. AUTOHARP PLAYS. ALL BEGIN A DANCE SINGING JOURNEY SONG. IN THE DANCE THEY MYSTERIOUSLY ADVANCE ON GERVASE AND CHUNTER APPEARING TO ATTACK THEM WITH THEIR FARM IMPLEMENTS. BUT INSTEAD THEY TAKE THEM INTO THEIR RANKS TO DANCE WITH THEM. DANCE STOPS. CHUNTER AND GERVASE STAND IN A WIDE CIRCLE OF PEASANTS.

GERVASE: Well Chunter, it seems that every man must find his own destiny. Every man must make what he can of his own life. You cannot change positions and expect to have changed lives. It is what is INSIDE you, that is the man, not the position you occupy in life. As Lumba taught us, the whip that is meant for you, falls on your back; and the life we are born to lead, we must lead.

CHUNTER: It would seem like it master.

GERVASE: Even you? Chunter.

CHUNTER: Even me master.

GERVASE: But we are now equals, brothers.

CHUNTER: I've been your friend, your bedmate, your beaten mate, your right-hand man, but I'm happier now, your servant again, so that I can marry my Amelia and lead my own life.

SINGING AND AUTOHARP CHORDS BACK CHUNTER'S SPEECH. EXITING:

And lead my own life I did. And lead his own life he did. And, as for travelling, he always seemed happiest by his own fireside. And, as for Church, like the rest of us he slept through every sermon.

THE END

Music for the play

JOURNEY SONG AND AUTOHARP CHORD BY JEFF PARTON

The full song consists of the sequence A, B, A.

Sir Gervase Becket, step forward.

FANFARE MUSIC BY STUART JOHNSON

Pages 1, 38-39 and 71: The opening and closing of Part One, and Gervase's descent from the gallows in Scene 25

Pages 16, 20 and 33: Hunting fanfare for before and after Scene 6, and the middle of Scene 11

Page 30: The arrival at the army camp in Scene 10

Pages 41 and 68: Solemn fanfare for the opening of Part Two and the march to the gallows, Scene 25

ou would like regular information
new Methuen plays, please write to
e Marketing Department
re Methuen Ltd
New Fetter Lane
ndon EC4P 4EE